Home Studio Handbook

written by Robert Scott

with photographs by Chris Burfoot
and Robert Scott

Published on behalf of
Courtenay Photographic Lighting
301-311 Rainham Road South
Dagenham Essex RM10 8DH

by
Ashdale Press
Ashdale House, 200 Lincoln Road
Peterborough PE1 2NQ

printed by
Hemmings & Capey, Leicester

ISBN 1 870899 01 6

CONTENTS

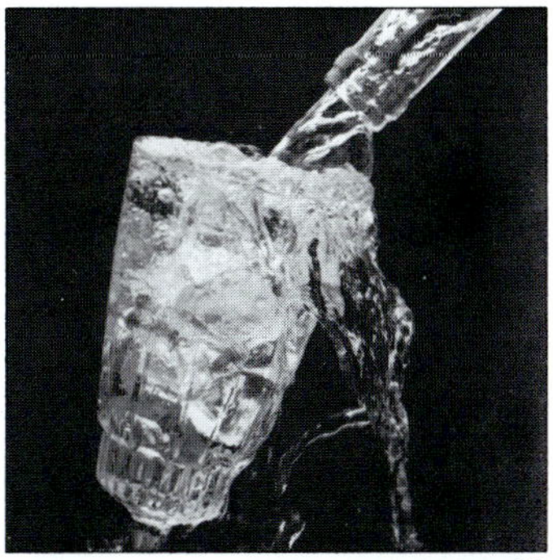

page 19

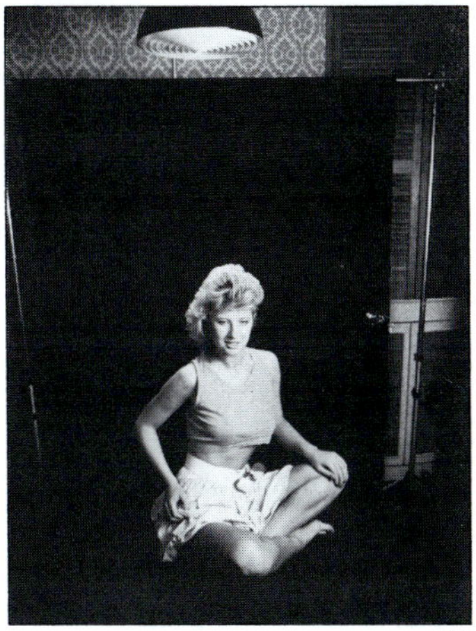

page 56

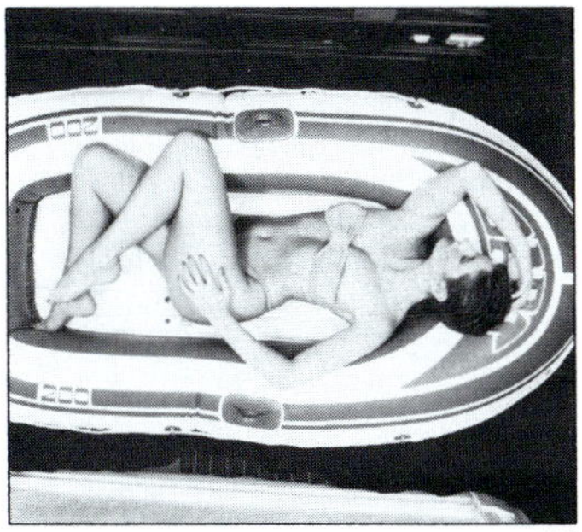

page 59

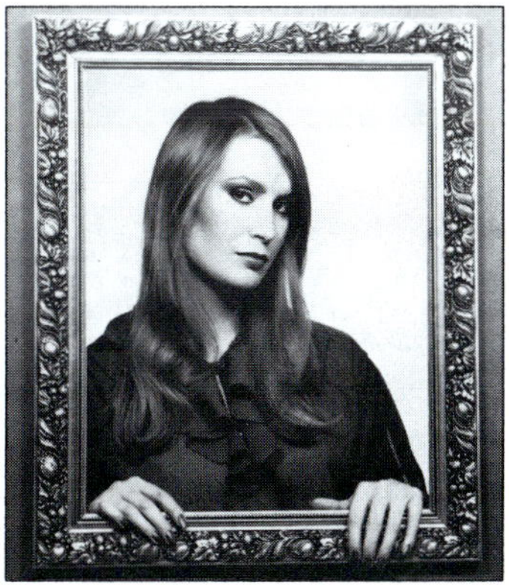

page 63

SHOOTING AT HOME

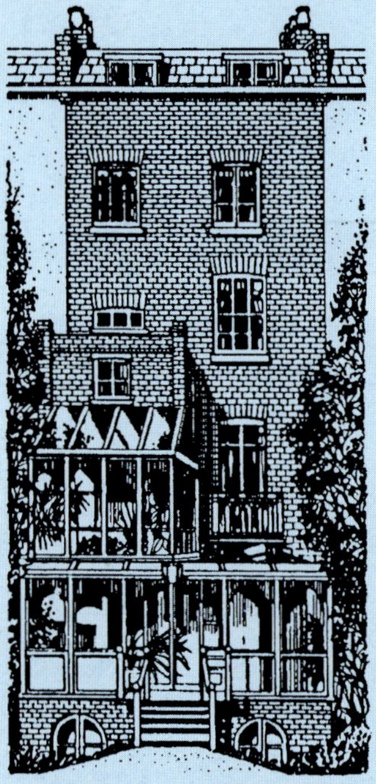

Almost any home has space for a home studio. You can get by with an area about 8 or 10 feet long and about 6 feet wide. Most home studios are temporary – you will have to pack all the equipment away after shooting. But take a fresh look at the attic, garage or basement – there may just be enough room for a permanent table-top studio, if nothing else.

Opposite:
You don't need a professional studio to shoot attractive head-and-shoulder portraits of friends and relations. Moving in close not only adds more impact to the picture, it also eliminates distracting surroundings.

Would you like to take top-quality studio photographs in your own home? It's not as difficult as you might think. You don't need a lot of space, or large amounts of expensive equipment. This book will show you how to work in different areas around an ordinary house, using a minimum of lighting and accessories to achieve excellent results. In most cases, the photographs will be indistinguishable from those taken in fully-equipped professional studios.

But why work at home when large, well-equipped studios are available for hire? It's not just a matter of saving money. You'll need to buy lighting equipment and accessories for shooting at home, so hiring a studio could be cheaper initially. However, it may not be so convenient. The studio may be some distance away. You will have to book in advance and work to fixed time periods, and you will have to clear everything away at the end of each session. And that's assuming you can find a suitable studio in your area.

Working at home is much more flexible. If necessary, you can spend a whole day arranging a single picture and you may even be able to leave your subject set-up until you have checked the results on the processed film. In addition, many subjects are best photographed outside a purpose-built studio. Portraits can benefit from a natural environment. Children are much more at ease in their own homes. Valuable works of art are safer with their owners close at hand.

At first sight, the average home does not appear to be the ideal place for a photographic studio. But that's because the term "studio" implies a large clear area. In fact, your "home studio" need be no larger than the space required for a tripod and a table. At most, you may need to move a few pieces of furniture and set up a support for a background.

The studio does not need to be in a room, either. The most unlikely areas of your house may have good photographic potential. There are advantages to shooting portraits halfway up a staircase, or in a doorway. And have you considered the possibilities of taking pictures in the attic or garage?

The studio equipment you need is very light and portable, so you can set-up and shoot in other homes, as well.

Almost all the photographs in this book have been taken in home studios. Yet some of them have the appearance of pictures from professional studio set-ups. The secret is to work within the limitations of the space available. It would be nice to shoot full-length portraits against large plain backgrounds, but this just isn't possible in most home studios. However, if you concentrate on head-and-shoulder pictures, a small studio area is all you need. Similarly, a small still-life arrangement will give you more successful pictures than a large set-up.

There are many ways to make the most of small studios areas, both in terms of the actual space, and the lighting techniques. As you read the following pages, keep in mind that most of the ideas are interchangeable with different subjects and set-ups. And remember that although a book can point you in the right direction, only practice will make you a better photographer.

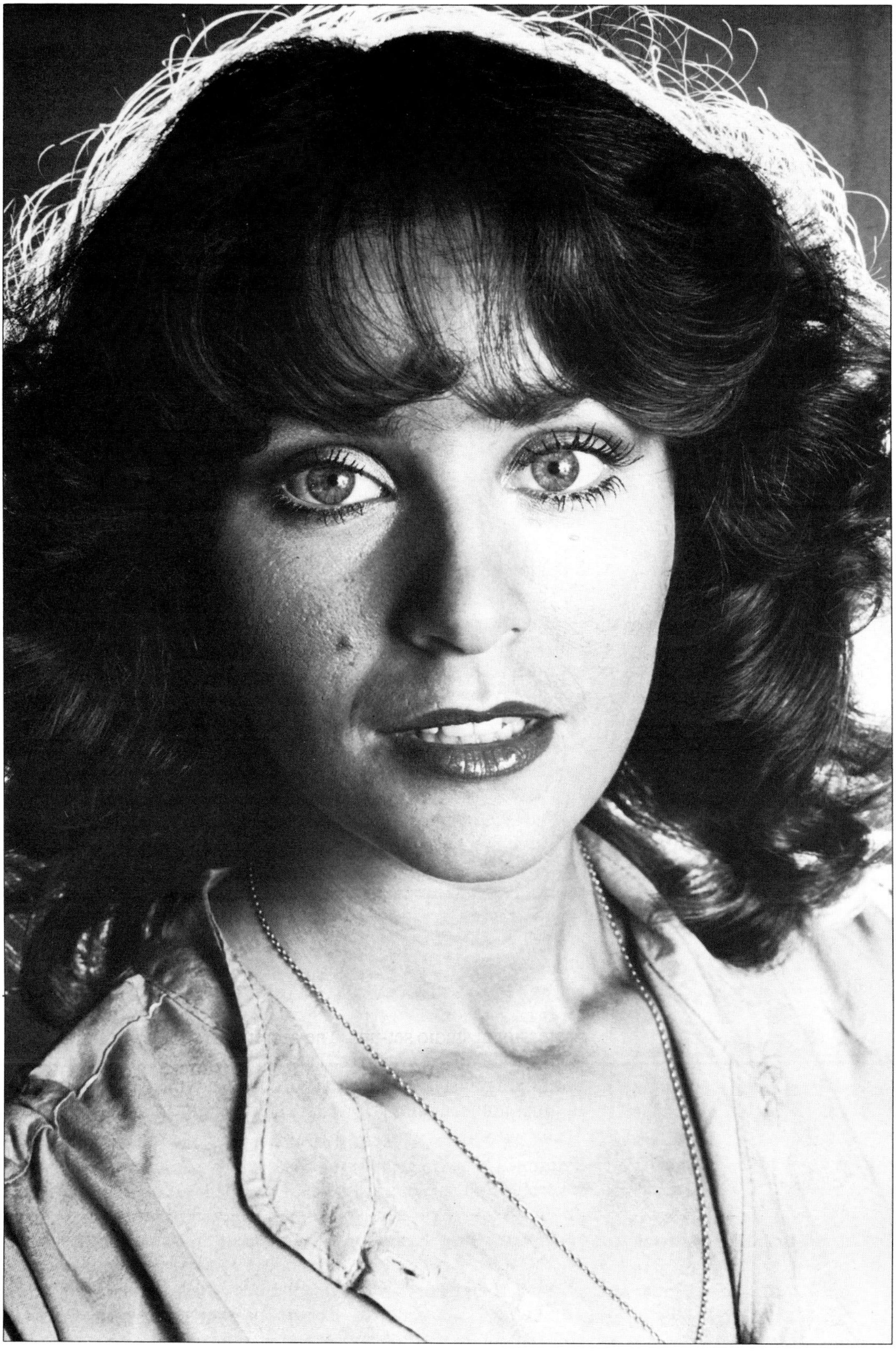

CAMERAS AND ACCESSORIES

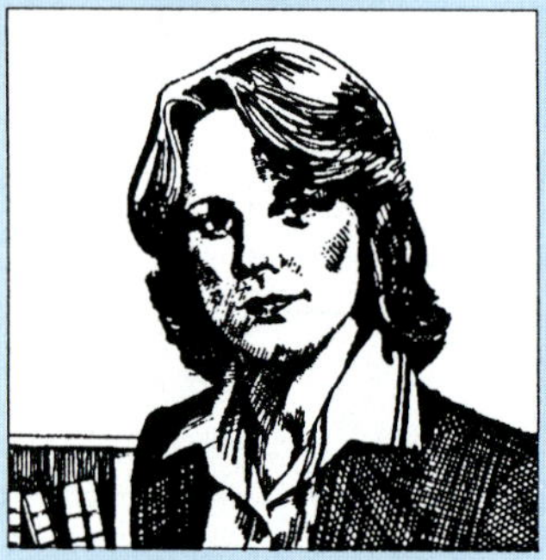

Non-reflex cameras are not really suitable for studio photography. At close working distances, what you see in the viewfinder (above) may not be what appears on the film (below).

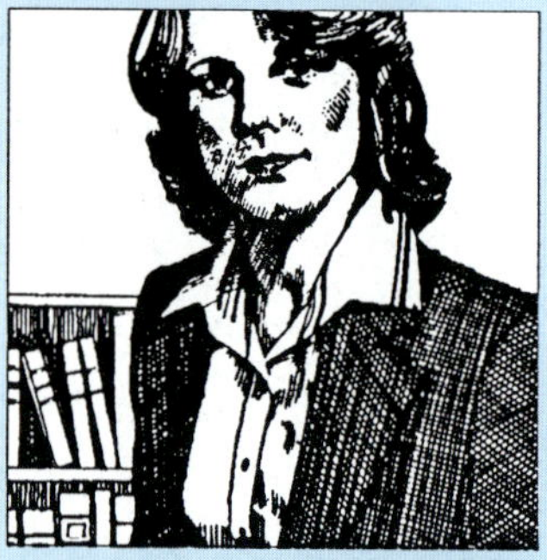

Reflex cameras overcome this problem by using the same lens both for viewing the subject and recording the image on film (it's all done by mirrors).

Home studio work needs a reflex camera, either single-lens or twin-lens. This is because you will often need to compose close subjects accurately in the viewfinder. Reflex cameras use the same or a similar lens for creating an image both in the viewfinder and on the film, so what you see in the viewfinder is what you get on the film (for most practical purposes).

Many photographers using a home studio will probably have a 35mm single-lens reflex camera. Almost every model is suitable for home shooting. If you are about to buy a 35mm camera for studio work, keep in mind that the requirements are fairly basic, and many of the least expensive models are just as good as top-of-the range models for this type of work. If you have a limited budget, it is much better to buy a basic camera and a couple of lenses than a more advanced camera with a single lens.

If money is less of a problem, it is worth considering a roll-film camera, either now or at some time in the future. One advantage is the larger format, which gives better quality prints and transparencies. But even more important for many roll-film users is the option of a waist-level viewfinder. This is especially useful when photographing people.

The choice of film is partly personal, partly practical. If you are shooting with tungsten light, a fast film (such as ISO 400) helps to maintain a mid-range aperture and shutter speed. With most flash systems, there should be sufficient power to obtain the better quality images given by a slower film (such as ISO 100). Try several makes of film before settling on one.

There isn't a 'best' lens for studio photography. It's simply a matter of choosing a lens, or lenses, best suited to the subject. The size of your shooting space may also affect your choice.

The standard camera lens (generally 50mm for 35mm formats; 75mm or 80mm for roll-film formats) will handle a wide variety of situations and allows the camera to be used fairly close to the subject (a big advantage in small areas). On the other hand, a close viewpoint can distort the perspective of the image.

If you can only afford one lens to begin with, a short telephoto (100mm or 135mm for 35mm cameras; 150mm for roll-film models) or a telephoto zoom lens will probably offer the best balance of the pros and cons.

One of the secrets of successful home studio photography is keep it simple. Some of the most striking shots are also likely to be some of the most straightforward. This means that camera accessories should only be used when they are absolutely essential.

A tripod is absolutely essential. With available light or tungsten lighting, it keeps the camera steady during exposures which can last several seconds. With studio flash, where the duration of the light is brief enough to 'freeze' camera movement, a tripod keeps the camera in a fixed position while you move around adjusting the set. A cable release is also very useful. So is a Polaroid back (if available for your camera). A filter can sometimes improve a picture.

And that's about it. Any spare money you have will probably be better spent on lighting equipment and accessories.

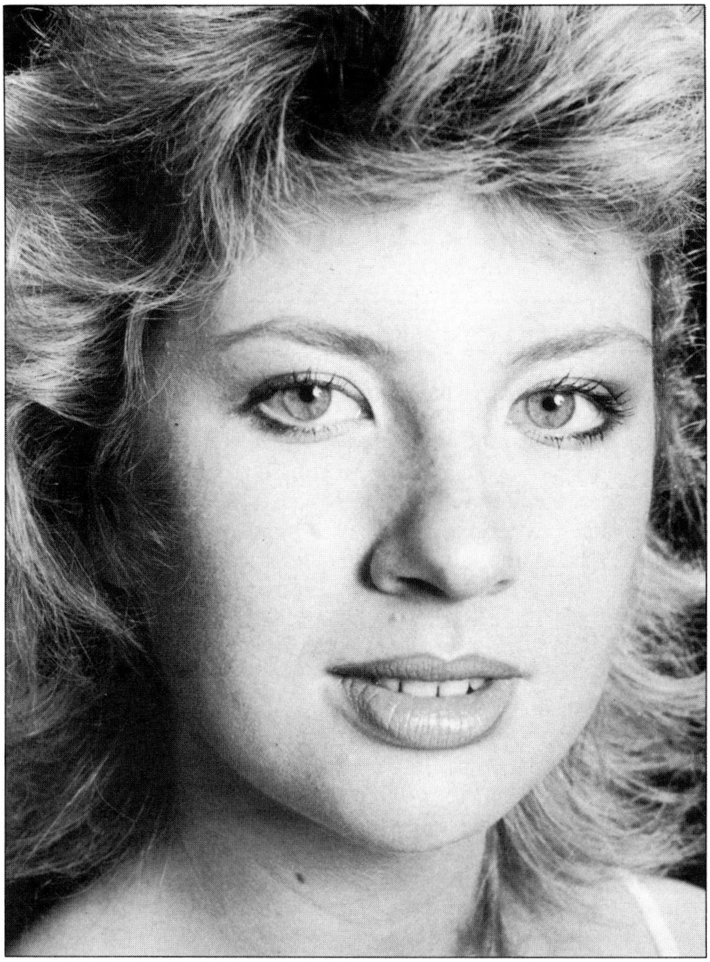

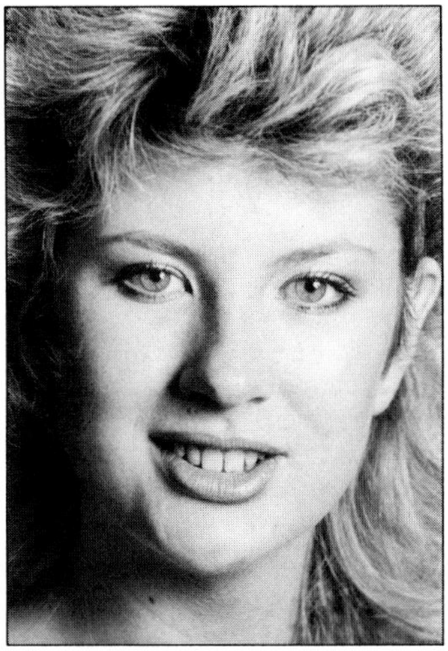

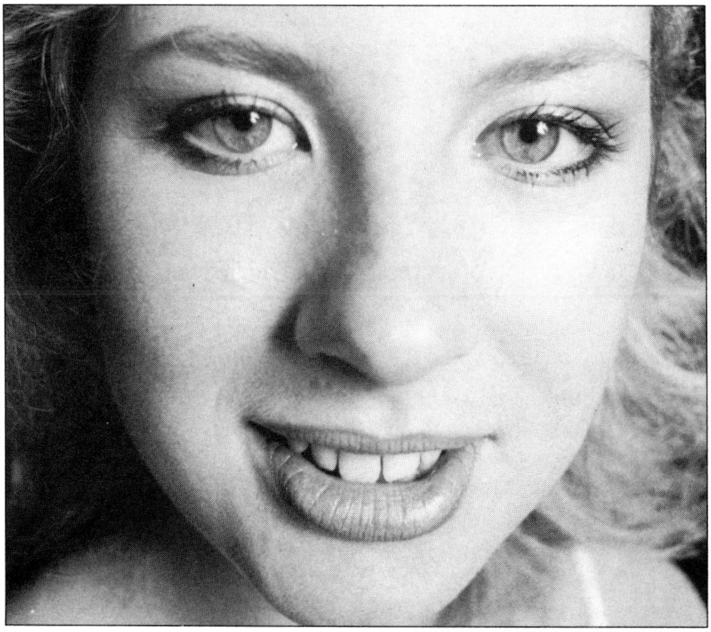

As a general rule, a portrait taken with a telephoto lens *(top left)* gives more pleasing results than a portrait taken with a standard lens *(above)*. In fact, it is not the focal length of the lens which affects the perspective of the image, but the distance between the lens and the subject. For a given distance, the perspective from both lenses will be identical. However, because the telephoto lens gives an enlarged image, you can generally use it from a greater distance. The telephoto shot was taken on a 35mm camera with a 70-210mm zoom lens set to 200mm, and a lens-to-subject distance of about 8 feet. The standard lens shot was taken with a 50mm lens on the same camera at a distance of about 3 feet from the subject. A good portrait lens for roll-film cameras is the 150mm. Wide-angle lenses are not suitable for head-and-shoulders shots, since the perspective produced by the short lens-to-subject distance distorts the features of the face *(bottom left)*.

SELECTING THE RIGHT FORMAT

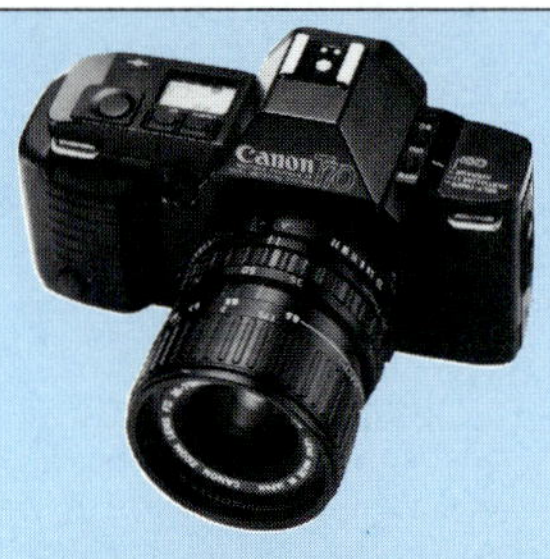

A 35mm single-lens reflex camera will be the first choice for many home-studio photographers. It offers good value, plus an extensive range of reasonably-priced accessories.

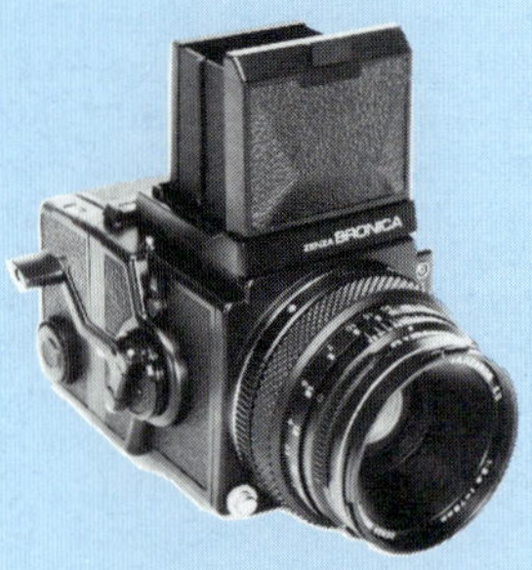

For 'serious' studio photography, a roll-film single-lens reflex camera is well worth considering. It's not much more expensive than a good 35mm reflex system, but offers many advantages in both shooting and selling the images.

Most photographers will tell you that a roll-film camera is better than a 35mm camera for studio work. Don't believe them. A roll-film camera is usually better, but there are advantages and disadvantages to both formats. Here are some of the arguments.

Roll-film cameras use a larger format than 35mm cameras, so image quality should be better. This is not usually noticeable in small prints, but enlargements over 10 x 8in should benefit. Roll-film transparencies are preferred by picture libraries, though more and more are now accepting 35mm slides for certain types of subject. If you are shooting for slide shows, 35mm slides will be required, but they don't have to be shot with a 35mm camera – some roll-film cameras accept 35mm film backs.

Exposure-for-exposure, film for roll-film cameras is more expensive than for 35mm cameras. However, many roll-film users discover that they tend to shoot fewer frames than when using the smaller format. 35mm films are available in lengths of 12, 15, 24, 27 and 36 exposures (though not all emulsions come in all lengths). 120 roll film gives 10, 12 or 15 exposures, depending on the camera format (see below). Some roll films are also available in 220 lengths, giving 20, 24 or 30 exposures.

It's not true that roll-film cameras are more expensive than 35mm cameras – it is the lenses which put your bank balance into the red. Before committing yourself to an attractive-looking roll-film camera and standard lens, check out the cost of the additional lenses and accessories which you might require over the next couple of years. Close-up equipment for roll-film cameras is particularly expensive – 35mm cameras offer much better value if you want to specialise in this area.

The big advantage of roll-film cameras is the waist-level viewfinder. Eye-level finders put the camera between you and the subject. With a waist-level finder, you only need to tilt your head to switch attention from the subject to the image. Many photographers find it easier to compose an image on a waist-level screen and it is also easier to build a rapport with portrait subjects.

There are three main roll-film formats – 6 x 4.5cm, 6 x 6cm and 6 x 7cm. The first offers the least expensive way into roll-film photography – but the waist-level finder can't be used for vertical format shots. The 6 x 6cm format is the most widely used. Being square, the camera is always used in an upright position, which makes life a lot easier. Recommended, if you can afford it. The 6 x 7cm format is ideal for studio work, especially portrait and glamour photography, but the cost will place it outside the range of most home studio users. With some 6 x 7cm cameras, the film back rotates for vertical format shots, rather than the whole camera. This retains use of the waist-level finder.

35mm cameras often have more advanced specifications than roll-film models. This isn't too important for studio photography, since only the basic features are used for most shots.

If the camera is not exclusively for studio photography, keep other applications in mind when you select the format. A 6 x 7cm camera is not ideal for Sunday afternoon nature rambles!

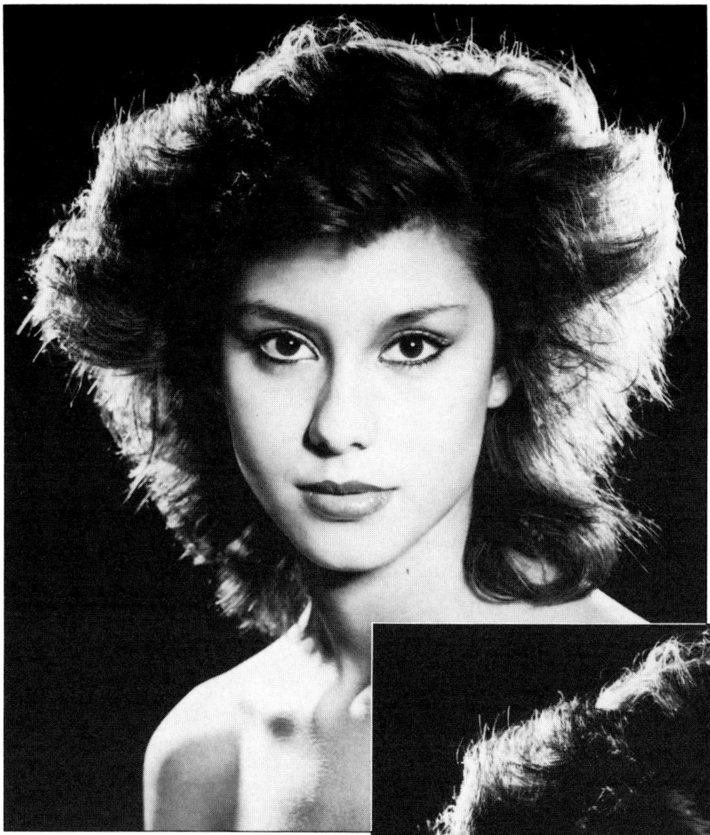

These prints indicate the range of film formats commonly available in single-lens reflex cameras. The pictures show the relative sizes of the formats – not their actual size. The smallest format is the 36 x 24mm frame (bottom right) given by cameras using 35mm film. The three formats from roll-film are 6 x 4.5cm, 6 x 6cm and 6 x 7cm. Many roll-film cameras can be used with different film backs to give different formats, including 35mm. Since few photographers print square pictures, a 6 x 6cm format does not offer any significant advantage over 6 x 4.5cm negatives in terms of quality – but the square format does allow the final framing to be done in the darkroom, rather than in the camera.

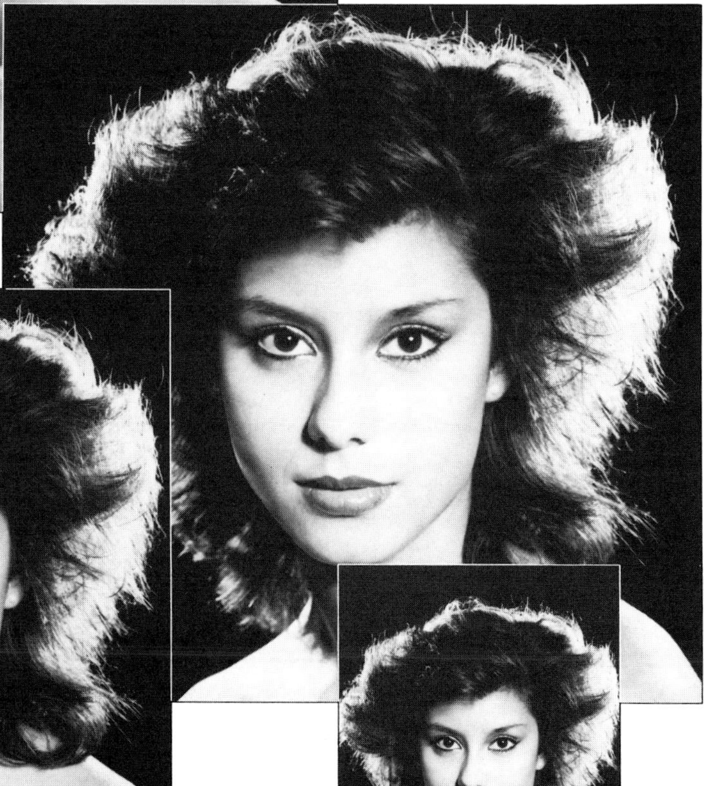

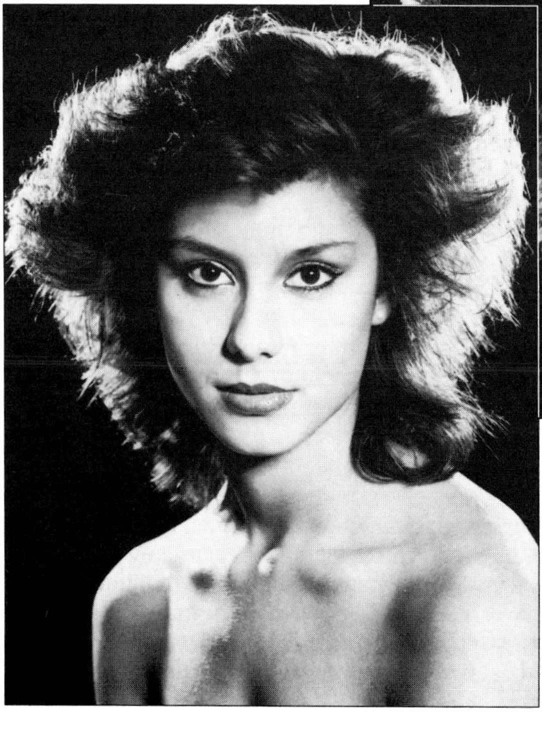

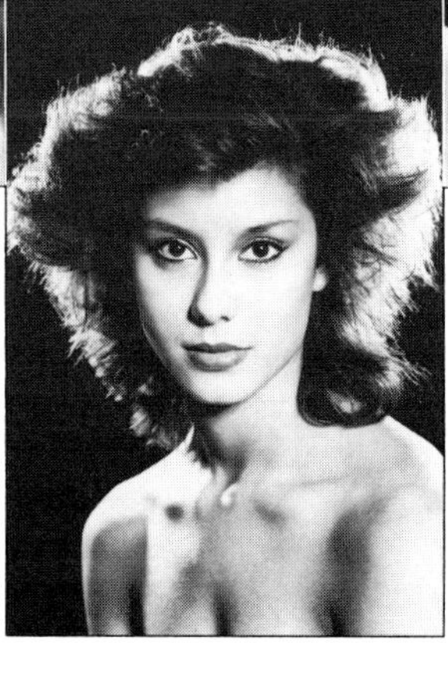

CHOOSING A STUDIO CAMERA

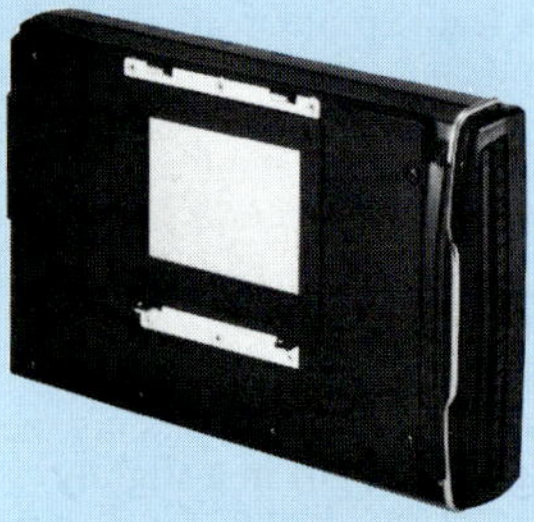

Most roll-film single-lens reflex cameras offer the option of a Polaroid Back. The back accepts Polaroid sheet film, which will give a black-and-white or full colour print within a minute or so of firing the camera shutter. This is invaluable for studio photography, since it enables you to check the lighting and exposure before changing to a film back for conventional film. No frames are lost when film backs are interchanged, even if you are only part-way through a roll film, so the Polaroid Back can be attached at any time during a studio session to check the image.

Polaroid backs are also available for some 35mm single-lens reflex cameras. However, because a fibre optic sheet is needed to transfer the image from the film plane to the print emulsion, they are very expensive and only worth considering for specialist applications.

You don't need an expensive state-of-the art camera for studio photography. The following list gives the basic requirements for a 35mm single-lens reflex:

– shutter speed range from 1 second to 1/500 sec; it must be possible to set these speeds manually;

– fully interchangeable lenses; it must be possible to set the lens aperture manually.

That's all! The other essential features are common to all cameras of the last 20 years and don't need to be considered when making your choice. Some other features can be useful; but many are not required. Here is a guide to help you select the best camera for your needs.

Through-the-lens metering. Can be useful if you are combining flash with daylight or tungsten light, though a separate hand-held exposure meter is often more convenient. Through-the-lens metering cannot be used with studio flash.

Flash synchronization. Almost every recent 35mm single-lens reflex camera has flash synchronization suitable for studio flash. However, there is an annoying trend for cameras to be manufactured without a standard co-axial flash socket. This is only a minor irritation, since the co-axial plug from studio flash units can be attached to the hot-shoe of such cameras via an inexpensive hot-shoe adaptor. Some recent cameras offer flash synchronisation at shutter speeds faster than the usual 1/60 sec. Studio flash should not be used with any camera at a shutter speed faster than 1/125 sec.

Multiple exposure control. By no means essential – but extremely useful. In addition to obvious effects, it can also be used to boost the effective power of your flash units. For example, if you want to shoot at a lens aperture of f/22 to obtain maximum depth-of-field for a table-top shot, you may find that a normal flash exposure will underexpose the film. However, by fixing the camera on a sturdy tripod and making several exposures on the same frame, you can build up the required density of image.

Automatic film advance. Appears to be a luxury – until you actually use a camera which winds the film on automatically after each exposure! It's particularly useful for portrait photography, since your subject will often relax after the first shot, and you can be ready to take the second shot almost immediately.

Battery check. Only a small feature, but since many cameras now rely on battery power for their operation, it's useful to be able to check the state of the batteries before and during a long studio session.

Autofocusing. Since most studio subjects don't move (or not much), and since your camera is on a tripod (isn't it?), the need for automatic focusing seems fairly limited. Autofocusing is becoming very sensitive in low light, and reaction times are down to around half-a-second or less, but no manufacturer is yet claiming 100% accuracy for every exposure. For general photography, autofocusing is proving very effective. By all means try it for studio work, but don't expect it to solve all your focusing problems. A manual override is essential.

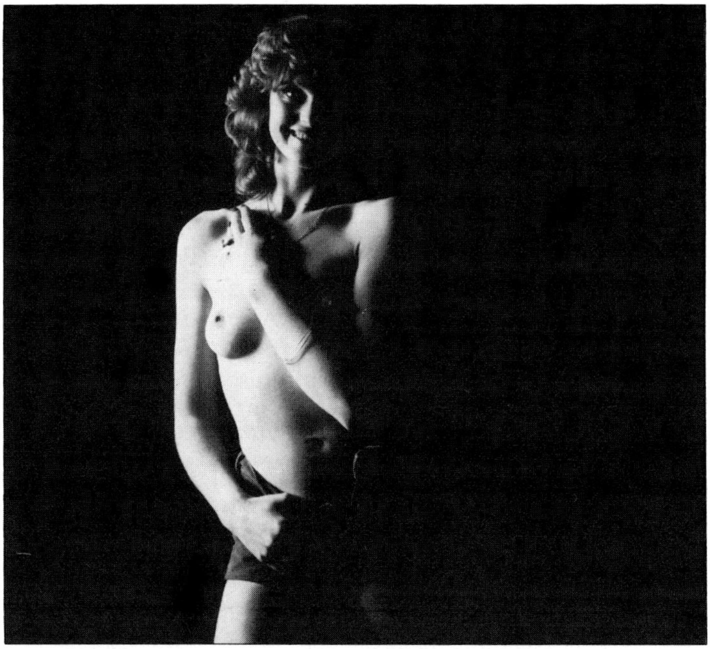

Multiple exposures can help you to make the most of your model – and your studio space. There is only one girl in the picture below, photographed four times on one frame of film. The picture on the left shows the image produced from a single exposure. Strong side lighting gives the shadows which avoid 'ghosting' in the overlapping areas. Only a small studio area is needed for this type of shot, since the girl does not move between exposures. It is the camera which turns, placing the image of the girl in a slightly different position on the film each time. The negative was taken with a roll-film camera, using a sheet of tracing paper over the focusing screen. To aid composition, an image was drawn on the paper each time the camera was moved.

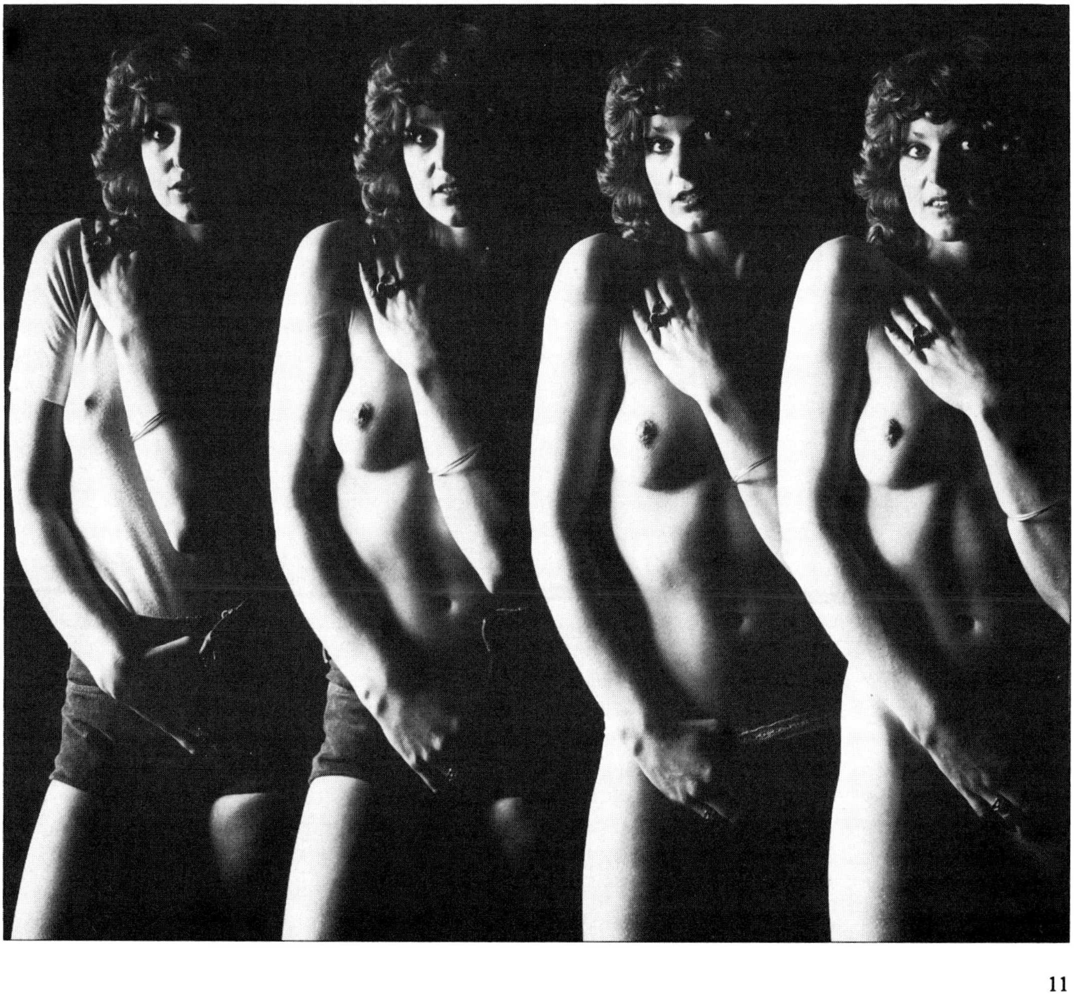

LIGHTING YOUR STUDIO

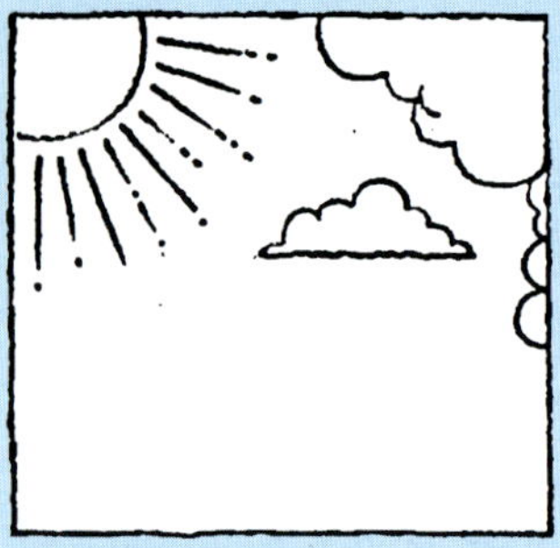

Many of the earliest portrait photographers used daylight studios. A bright, soft northern light is ideal for much studio work, but the weather is too variable for you to rely on this type of illumination.

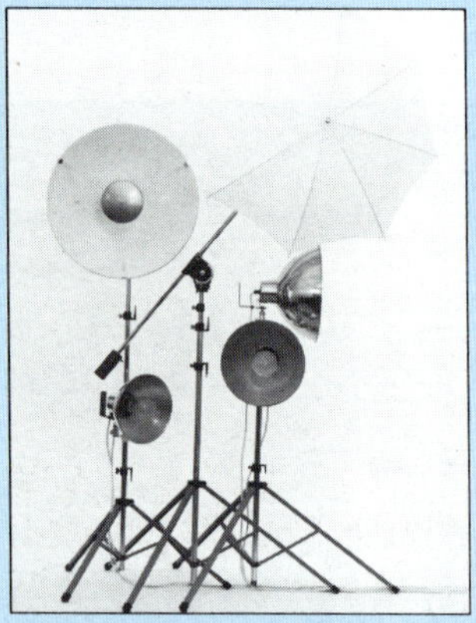

Tungsten lamp reflectors are available in a range of different shapes and sizes. For portrait work, you need the largest metal reflector you can find. Make sure it has a central metal bulb cover, so that only reflected light reaches the subject. If storage is a problem, use a white nylon brolly reflector. The smaller metal reflectors are more suitable for effect lighting.

The simplest and cheapest form of lighting for your home studio is daylight. And it can be very effective, providing you are able to shoot during the day, and can wait for the right weather to take your pictures.

Daylight is excellent for portraits. If you can find a north-facing window on a bright day, you will have a beautiful soft illumination that flatters the subject. If you have to use a window facing the sun, a net curtain hung over the frame will soften the light to give a similar effect.

A daylight studio is surprisingly versatile. By moving camera and subject in relation to the window, a wide range of different lighting effects is possible. And with a simple background sheet to hide any distractions in the room, plus a white reflector sheet to bounce light back into the shadow areas, you can produce results which equal anything taken with studio lighting. Unfortunately, daylight is neither consistent nor reliable. If you want to shoot at a time of your own choosing, you need artificial lighting for your studio.

There are two basic types of artificial studio lighting – tungsten and flash. Tungsten illumination can be obtained from photoflood bulbs. These are rather like domestic light bulbs, but they are overrun to give more light. Ratings are usually 275 watts or 500 watts, compared with the normal 60 watt or 100 watt bulbs in your lightshades and desk lamps. Because they are overrun, these bulbs don't last long – a couple of hours for the smaller bulbs; maybe six to eight hours for the larger bulbs. The working life can be extended by running the bulbs at low power while setting up a shot, switching them to full power for a few seconds while the exposure is made.

There are several disadvantages to tungsten lighting for the small studio. Although the light looks very bright when the bulbs are on full power, exposures for ISO 100 film require a disappointing slow shutter speed at quite a wide lens aperture – 1/30 sec at f/2.8 is not uncommon. And tungsten lamps are highly inefficient – they generate a tremendous amount of heat, as well as light. In a small studio area, this heat can quickly build up, making the working conditions unpleasant. Add to this the fact that you need colour film specially balanced for tungsten light, or daylight film with a filter which absorbs some of the light, and you have a set-up which is far from ideal.

A variation on tungsten lighting is the tungsten-halogen lamp. This is the type of bulb now used in most slide projectors – very small, but giving off a lot of light. Most tungsten-halogen lamps designed for photography are intended for video work. They use 1000 watt lamps, and some units run with two bulbs side-by-side. So much heat is generated that a fan is needed to keep the unit cool. Tungsten light photography is making a comeback in some professional studios in the form of tungsten-halogen units, but the system is not recommended for the small studio.

Video photography requires a bright, continuous light source. Still photography doesn't. What's needed is a very bright light that lasts for no more than the duration of the film exposure. Electronic flash is the answer.

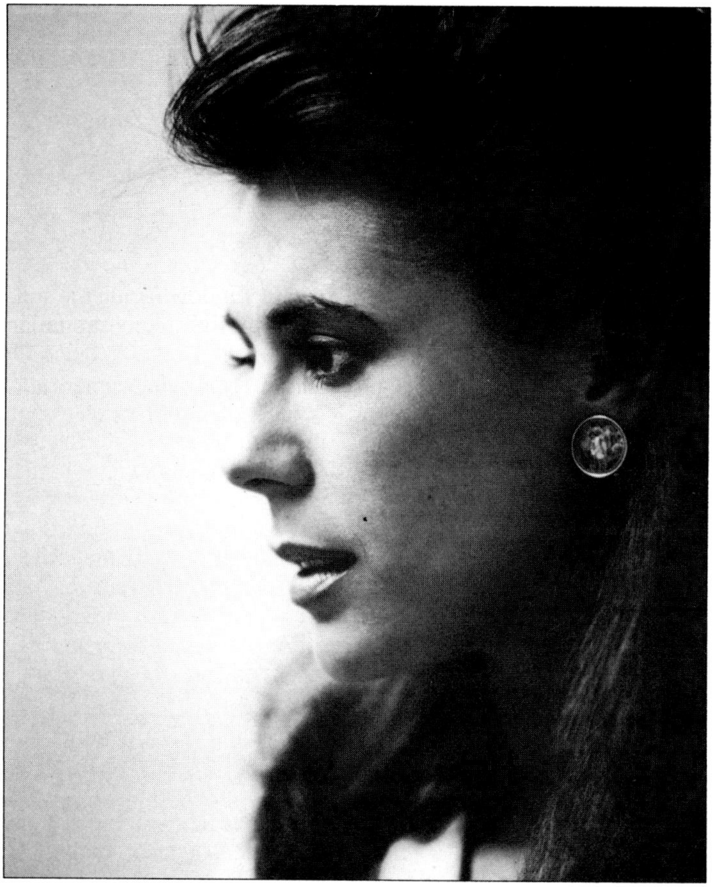

Left: Window light can turn any well-lit room into a portrait studio. Daylight is perfect for portraits, giving a quality of illumination which is difficult to match with any other form of lighting. However, unless you are working on a sunny day, the brightness of the light may be low. This picture was taken with a shutter speed of 1/15 sec and an aperture of f/2.8. A distracting background has been eliminated by positioning a white projector screen behind the subject.

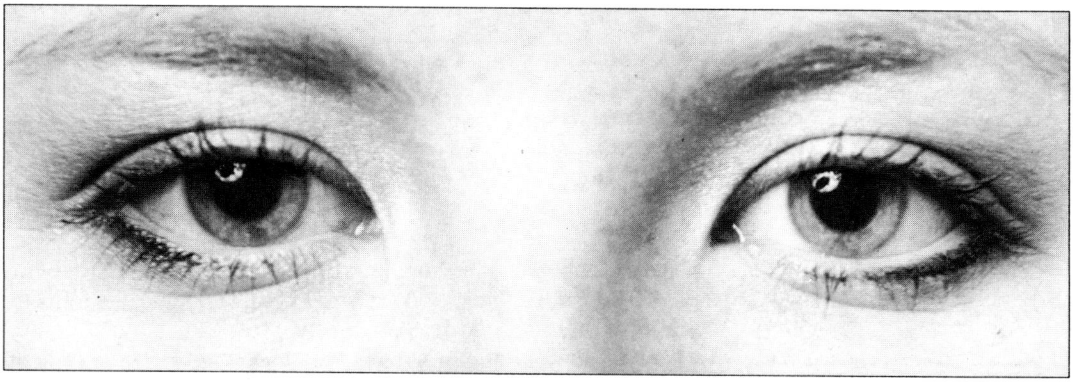

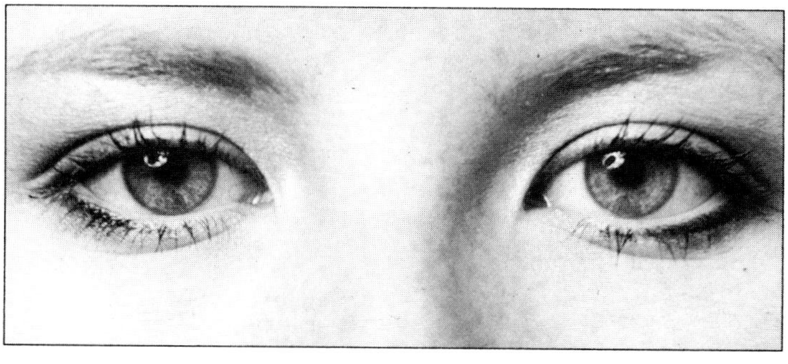

A less obvious disadvantage of tungsten or video lamps is the effect the bright light has on the pupils of the eyes. They contract (left). Research has shown that a person viewing portraits is attracted more strongly by eyes with wide pupils (above). The widest pupils are obtained by working in dim lighting with flash – the eyes do not have time to react to the light before the exposure is made.

ELECTRONIC FLASH

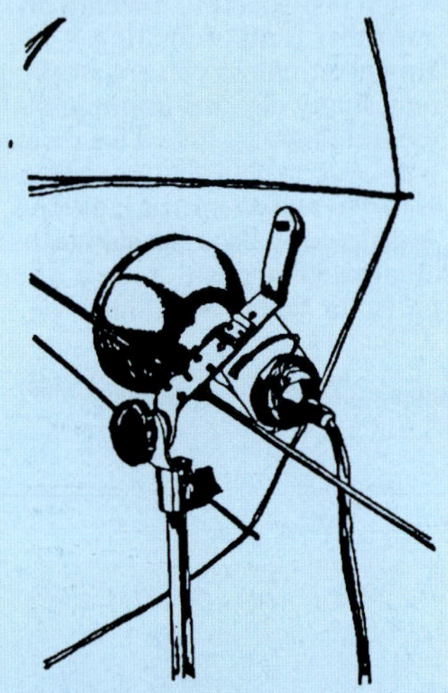

The Courtenay Brolly-Flash provides a bracket to take a battery flashgun, a tungsten reflector lamp and a brolly reflector. The bracket fits an adjustable stand. You attach the flashgun facing into the brolly to give diffuse lighting which is ideal for portrait photography, still-life work and close-ups. The tungsten lamp gives a fairly accurate guide to the effect of the lighting before you take a picture. Although the system has limitations, it offers an excellent introduction to studio flash photography. The Brolly-flash outfit consists of the bracket, stand and brolly. The tungsten lamp is not supplied, but can be bought at any good electrical shop. The stand and the brolly are part of the standard Courtenay studio flash system, so only the bracket becomes redundant if you upgrade.

Most photographers are familiar with electronic flash. Almost every camera accepts a small clip-on flashgun, making it possible to take well-exposed pictures in conditions which might otherwise require exposure times of a minute or more. Unfortunately, the camera is just about the worst possible place for the flashgun. We only accept the flat, lifeless images produced because of the convenience of the system.

Some flashguns have tilting heads, so that illumination can be reflected onto the subject. This can give better results, since the reflected light is more diffuse than the direct flash, giving softer shadows. And since the light is now reaching the subject at an angle to the camera, the shadows are more pronounced and this defines the shape of the subject. Many flash instruction booklets suggest bouncing the light off a ceiling when photographing people. This is wrong. Unless you are working in ideal conditions, the light will come down at too great an angle, throwing shadows under the eyes of the subject. It's much better the bounce the flash off a white wall, so that the flash reaches the subject from the side. This not only avoids the shadows under the eyes, it also offers a much more versatile system. By moving the position of the subject and flashhead, you can have the light reaching the face from a variety of angles.

It would be a lot easier, of course, if you could keep the subject and your camera in fixed positions, and move the white wall and the flashgun. This is possible if you substitute a lightweight reflector for the wall. Even with the flashgun still attached to the camera, bouncing the light off a reflector begins to open up a range of possibilities. An even wider range of effects is possible if the flashgun is removed from the camera and reconnected via a flash extension lead. The flashgun can now be moved some distance from the camera and positioned closer to the reflector for more efficient illumination.

A problem with camera flashguns is that you can't see the effect of the illumination until the film is processed. Unless, that is, you fix a tungsten reflector lamp next to the flashgun. The illumination from this lamp will be bounced from the lightweight reflector in the same way as the flash, so studying the areas of light and shade thrown on the subject by the lamp should give a good impression of the final result. For convenience, you can buy a unit which fits the reflector, flashgun and tungsten lamp on a single stand via a metal bracket. Used within its limitations, this system can give results indistinguishable from pictures taken using more expensive units.

There are two main limitations to the system. First, many camera flashguns are not powerful enough for anything that needs the reflector more than three or four feet from the subject. It's often necessary to work at apertures of f/4, or even f/2.8. Second, camera flashguns take up to eight or ten seconds to recycle between exposures, even with fresh batteries. Recycling times of 20 or 30 seconds are common as the batteries become exhausted.

So although a reflector and camera flash unit is a good way to start with studio photography, you really need proper studio flash units if you are going to make the most of your home studio.

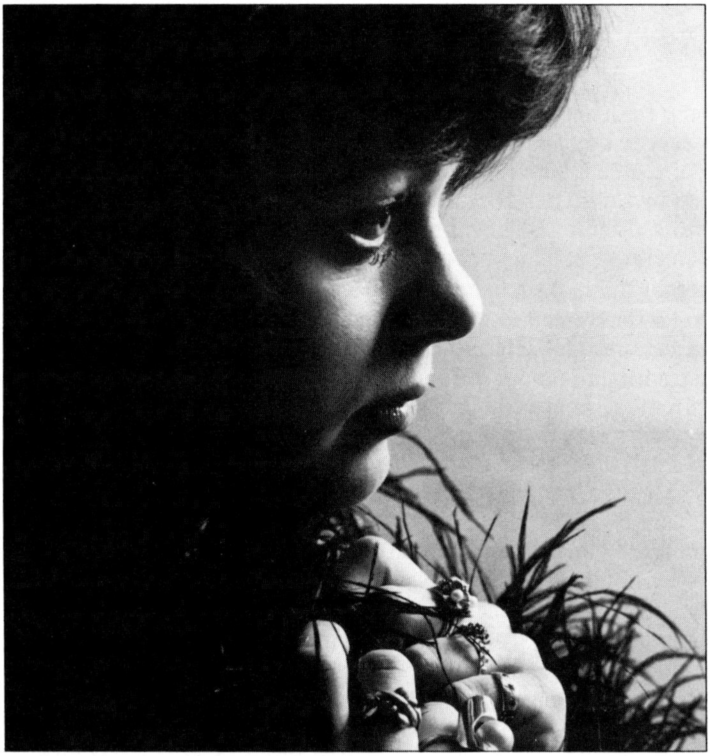

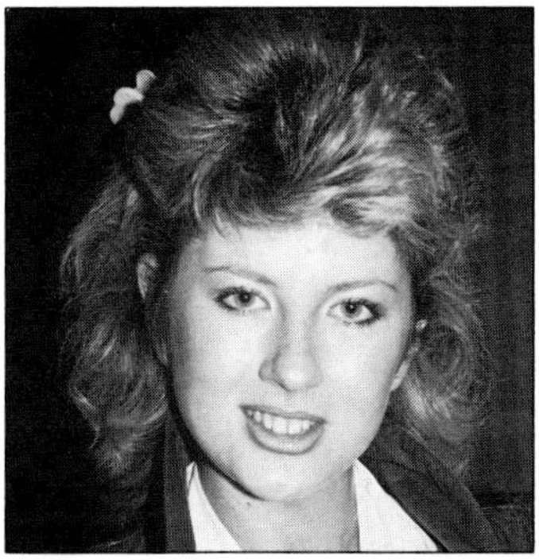

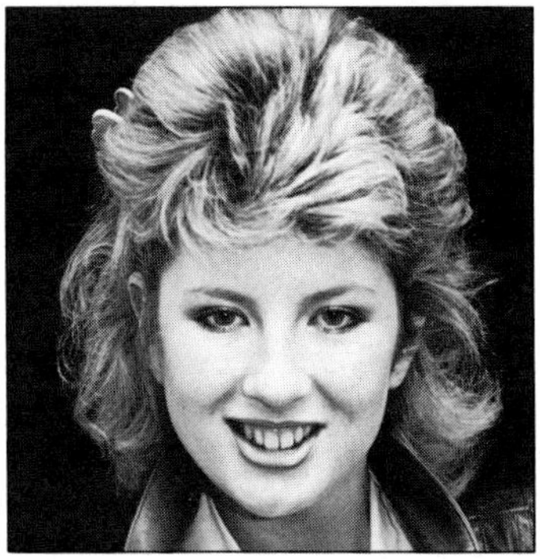

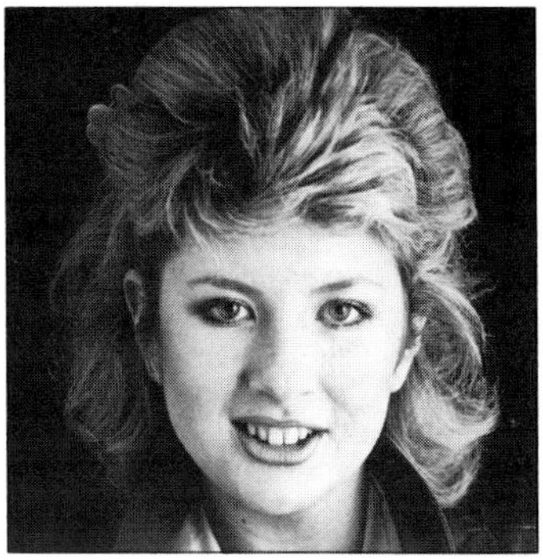

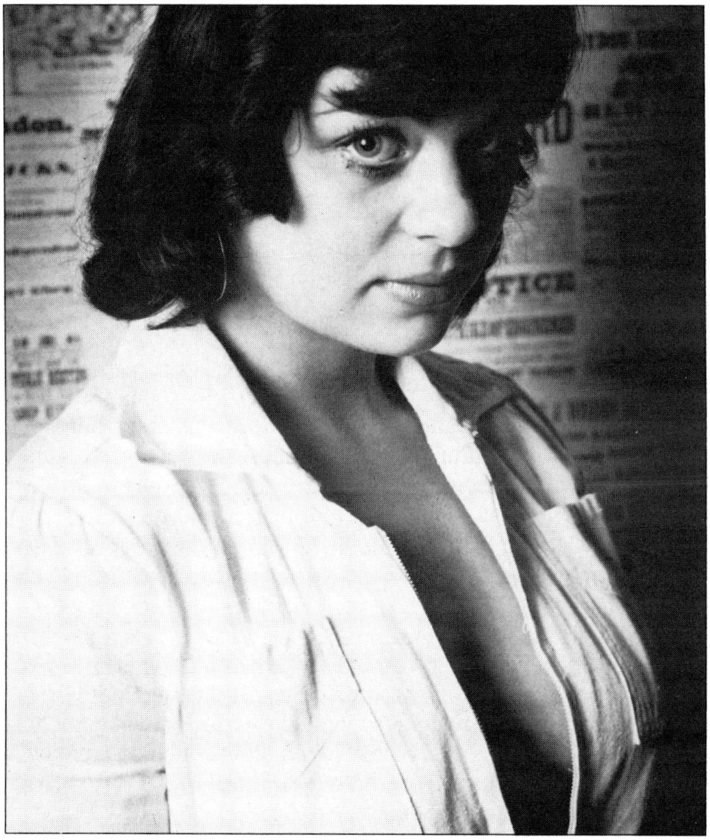

Above: An ordinary battery flashgun used on the camera gives unattractive flat, contrasty lighting *(above top)*. Bouncing the light off the ceiling improves the illumination, but can give dark shadows under the eyes *(above centre)*. Bouncing the light off the wall is the best way to make use of a tilt-and-swivel head flashgun fixed to the camera *(above bottom)*.

Left: Both the pictures on the left were taken with a single Brolly-flash unit fitted with a simple battery flashgun. Many more effects like these are possible by altering the position of the flash.

STUDIO FLASH

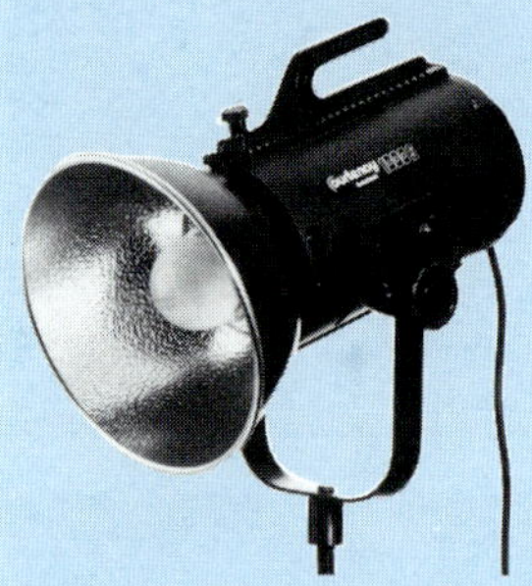

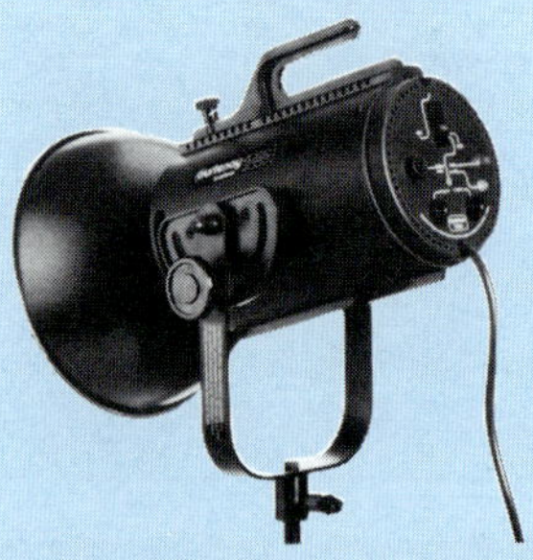

A studio flash unit may look difficult to use, but it is far simpler to operate than many modern battery flashguns. Units come in various sizes – the larger models are generally more powerful and offer extra features. However, for most home studios, the basic units will be more than adequate. You will obtain much more interesting results from two of three simple flash units than from one expensive model.

Opposite:
Your home studio does not need to be a large room – a small subject only requires a corner of a small room. But whatever the space you have available, studio flash will help you to produce quality results.

Studio flash is the ideal lighting for home shooting. It's easy to set up, easy to use, and can be packed away on top of the wardrobe, or under the bed, between sessions. Some photographers are intimidated by studio flash because it appears different to anything they have used before. But if you take a close look at a unit, you'll see that it is made up of a number of familiar items.

Most studio flash units are now self-contained. At the back is a box containing the electronics and the controls. At the front is a concave metal reflector. At the rear of the reflector is the flash tube. This is usually curved to form a circle, giving more efficient light distribution. In principle, the flash tube operates in much the same way as the tube in flashguns which sit on top of your camera. But battery flashguns start off with a slow recycling time, and this gets worse as the batteries lose power. Studio flash overcomes this problem by using mains power. The unit can be connected to any standard 13amp socket. This gives a recycling time of under 2 seconds. And since the mains power remains constant, the recycling time is always the same.

Immediately in front of the flash tube is a tungsten lamp. This provides the 'modelling' light – the light which helps you set up the unit to give just the right highlights and shadows. Since the modelling light is in the same position as the flash tube, the lighting effects you see before you take a picture should be almost identical to those produced by the flash on the film. The lamp is generally a 100 watt domestic light bulb. Special lamps are not needed, since the tungsten illumination is not used to form an image on the film.

The metal reflector at the front of some studio flash units is interchangeable. Different sizes and shapes of reflector alter the quality and concentration of the light. This is useful, but not essential, since the quality of the light can be controlled by the use of separate sheet reflectors. The metal reflectors of the least expensive studio flash units are usually fixed.

Controls on the simplest studio flash units can be nothing more than an on/off switch and a test button. The switch turns on both the flash circuits and the modelling lamp. On the rare occasions when you might want to work without a modelling lamp, you simply remove the bulb. The test button fires the flash. If you are using a single flash unit, the test button is not really needed. Its main purpose is to check synchronization when two or more units are being fired simultaneously.

As you move up the range of studio flash, more controls are found. Many units offer separate switches for the flash and the modelling light. And there is often a switch which alters the power of the flash, giving full, half and even quarter strength settings.

Some studio flash units have built-in 'slave cell'. This is a light-sensitive switch which reacts to the flash from another unit and fires its own flash in sympathy. A slave is very useful for multiple flash set-ups, since it saves having to connect the various units by cable. Plug-in slave cells can often be used with units which do not have them built in. There is little point in having a slave cell in the first unit you buy, since it will rarely be used.

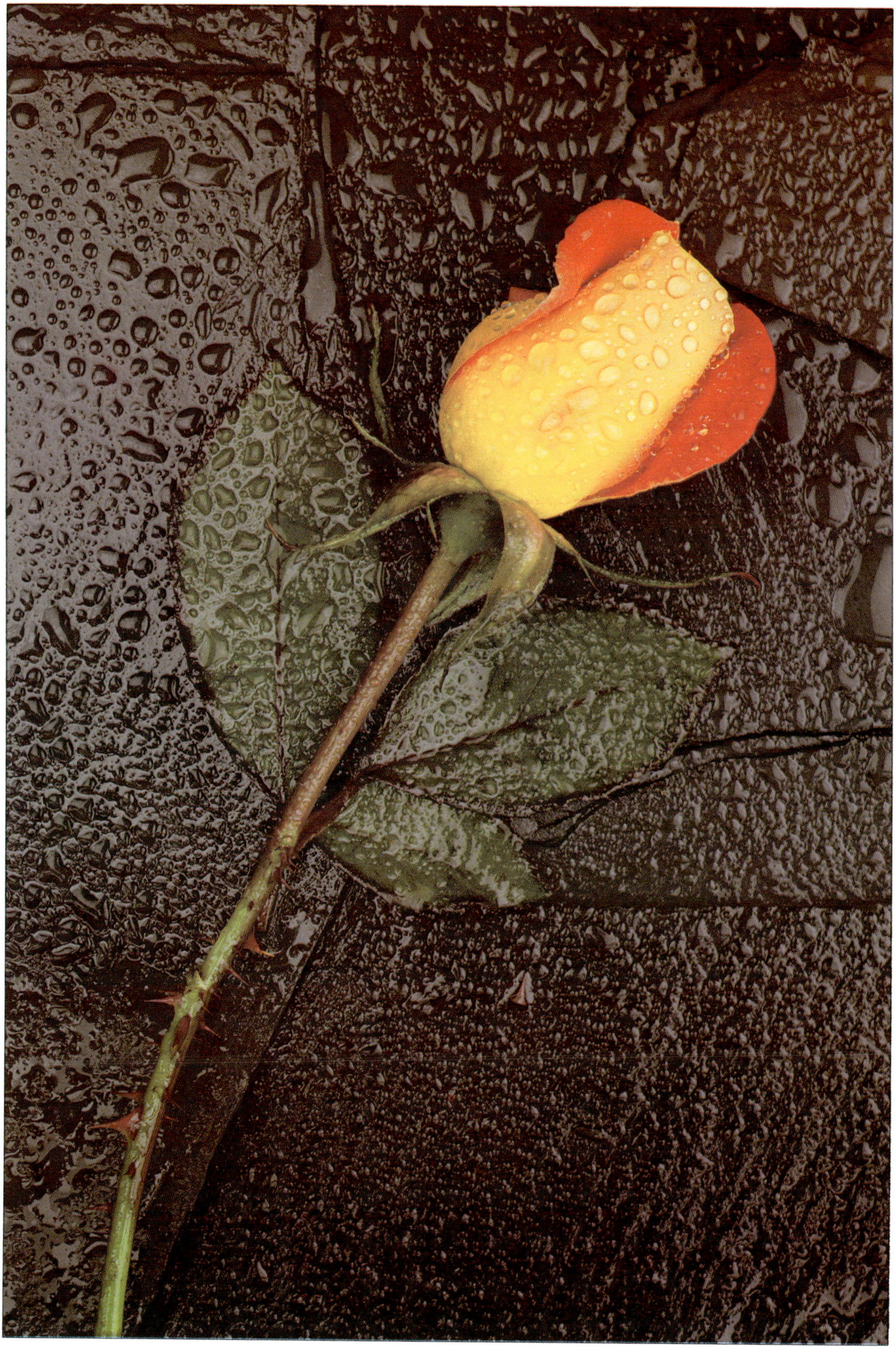

FLASH SYNCHRONIZATION

A focal plane shutter, as fitted to most 35mm single-lens reflex cameras, consists of two blinds which travel across the back of the camera, just in front of the film frame. The speed at which these blinds travel is constant – the effect of different shutter speeds is obtained by increasing or decreasing the delay between the first and second blinds. With fast shutter speeds, the delay is so short that the second blind starts to move before the first blind has reached the end of its movement (first diagram). At these speeds, the film is never completely uncovered at any time during the exposure.

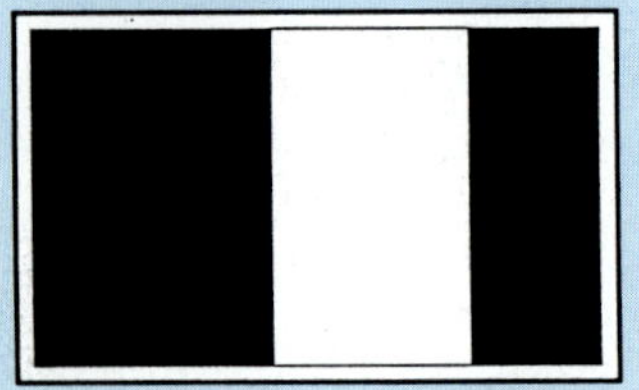

Shooting with studio flash at these faster speeds will produce a partially exposed frame of film. It is only at slower speeds that the first blind reaches the end of its travel before the second blind starts to move (second diagram).

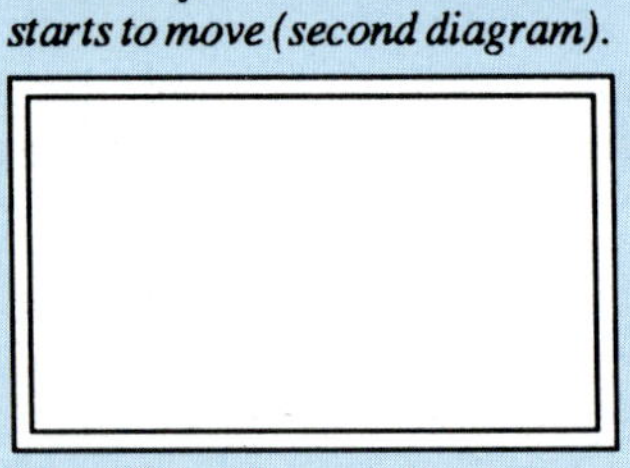

If the flash fires at the moment the first blind stops moving, all of the film will be exposed to the short duration of light. Some recent cameras allow flash synchronization at focal plane shutter speeds up to 1/250 sec. However, the fastest recommended speed for effective studio flash synchronization is 1/125 sec, and on many cameras, you need to set 1/60 sec. Check your camera instruction booklet carefully to make sure you are setting the correct speed.

Every camera has a flash synchronization circuit. Essentially, it is a simple make-and-break contact which comes together at the moment the shutter is wide open. To fire a flash so that the light reaches the film through the open shutter, you must connect the unit to the camera. With small battery flashguns, this is done automatically when you slide it into the camera accessory shoe. Metal pins at the base of the flashgun make connect with metal contacts on the camera. Accessory shoes with these contacts are called 'hot-shoes'.

Studio flash units don't have hot-shoe contacts. Since they are designed to be used some distance from the camera, connection is by means of a flash synchronization cable. One end of the cable is fitted with a large jack plug. This pushes into a socket on the back of the flash unit. The other end of the cable is fitted with a standard 3mm co-axial plug. This connects to a matching socket on the camera. The connections are often referred to as the PC plug and PC socket. Over recent years, quite a few cameras have been introduced without the PC socket. At first sight, this makes them impossible to use with studio flash. However, these cameras all have hot-shoes, and you can buy a hot-shoe adaptor which slides into the shoe and provides the required PC socket.

The PC plug and socket is the weakest link of any flash system. If the flash does not fire when you press the camera shutter release, the fault is almost certain to be a poor connection at the camera. In some cases, you'll find that the lead has fallen out. Other times, it will just need pushing in more tightly. The PC plug has adjustable 'jaws' which can be closed by gripping them with a pair of pliers. Don't apply much pressure with the pliers or you will distort the end of the plug and ruin it. Sometimes the connection stops working for no apparent reason. Always keep at least one spare flash synchronization lead — you'll need it.

The camera must be set to the correct synchronization speed. This is particularly important for camera which have focal plane shutters (most 35mm single-lens reflex models). You need the 'X-synchronization' shutter speed. This is usually given in the camera instruction booklet, and may also be marked on the shutter speed dial. Many battery flashguns now set the correct shutter speed automatically. This does not happen with studio flash. You must set the shutter speed manually.

Cameras with between-lens shutters can be set for flash synchronization at any shutter speed. This applies to many roll-film cameras. However, 1/125 sec is recommended as the fastest speed for use with studio flash. This is because studio flash units do not fire quite as quickly as small battery flashguns. At faster shutter speeds, the exposure could be over before all the light from the studio flash had reached the film.

When you are connecting the synchronization cable to the back of the studio flash unit, you will find that there are two suitable sockets. Both are identical and you can insert the plug into either. The additional socket is for running a cable to a second flash unit, giving multiple flash synchronization in situations where slave cells are not suitable.

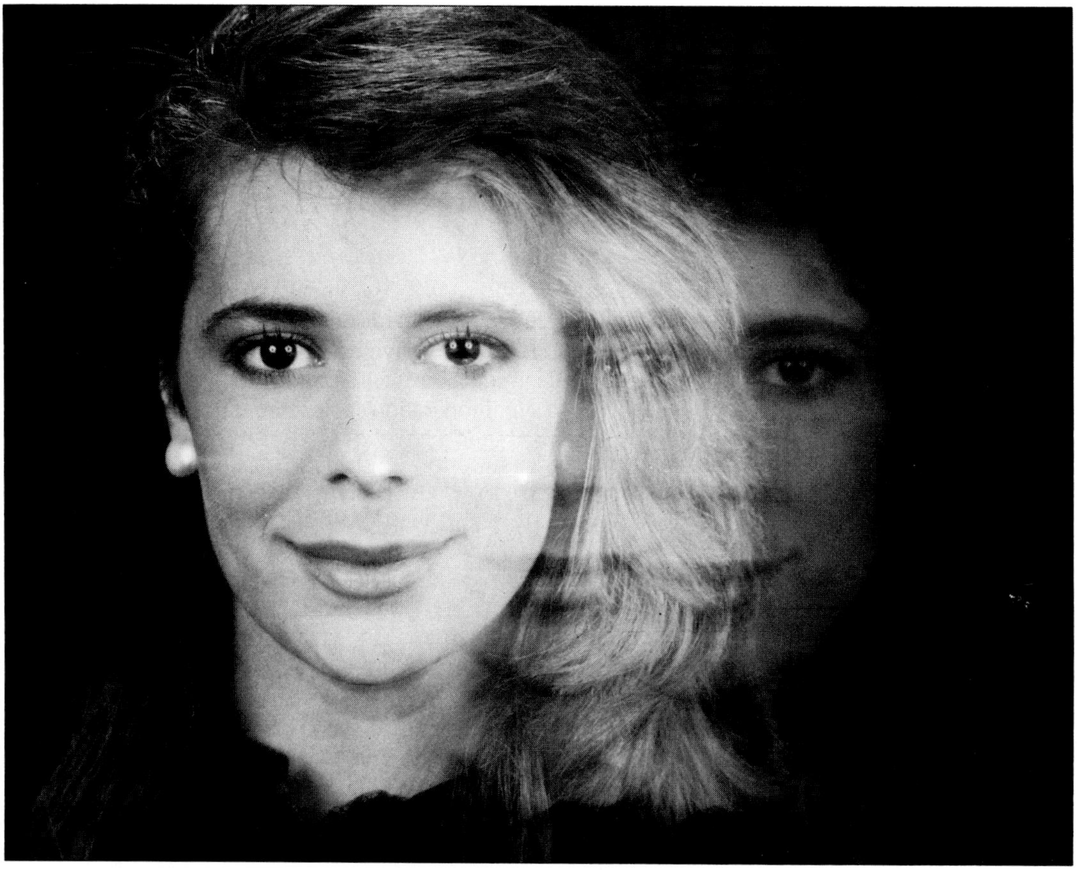

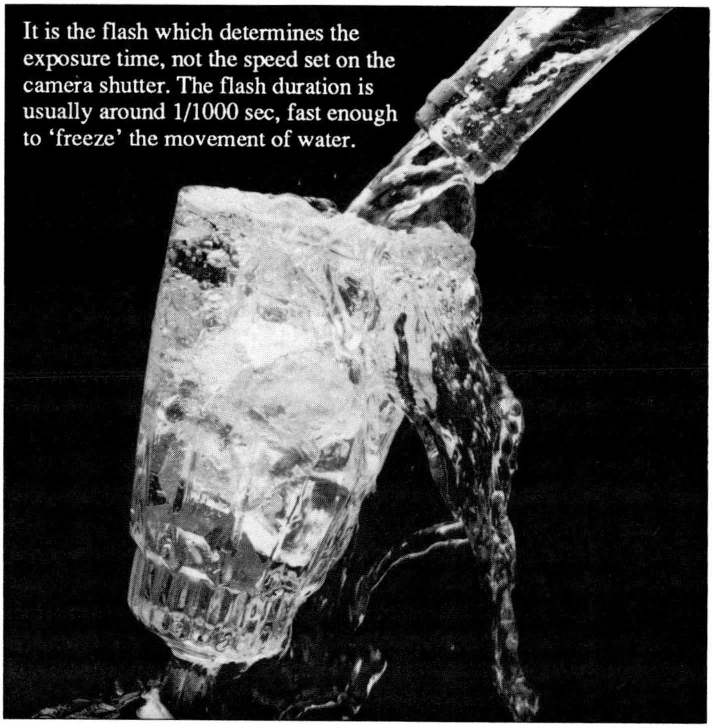

It is the flash which determines the exposure time, not the speed set on the camera shutter. The flash duration is usually around 1/1000 sec, fast enough to 'freeze' the movement of water.

Above: Interesting effects are possible by combining the flash exposure with an available light exposure. The flash exposure is over in around 1/1000 sec, and this brief duration will 'freeze' subject movement. The main image in this photograph is from a studio flash exposure. But rather than using the normal flash synchronization speed of 1/125 sec, the camera was set to a shutter speed of 4 seconds. Immediately the shutter release was pressed, the shutter opened and the flash fired. During the remainder of the 4 second exposure, the camera was moved two or three times, using the rotating head of a tripod to keep the lens level. The 'ghost' images which appear are the result of exposure to the flash modelling light which is illuminating the subject. If you like this type of effect, be prepared to shoot 20 or 30 exposures to obtain one or two acceptable images.

USING A SINGLE FLASH

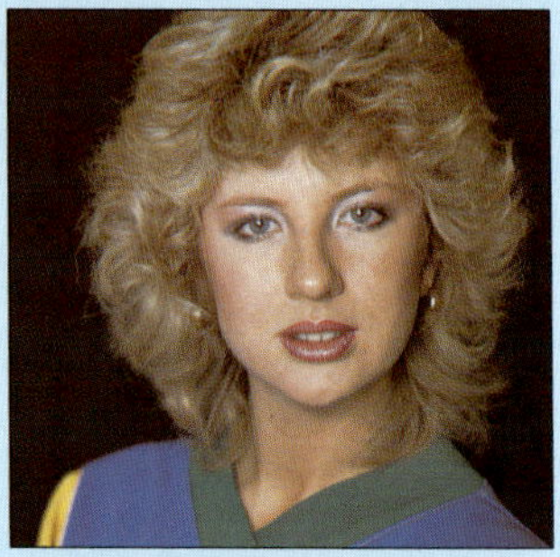
Light close to the lens axis and at camera height.

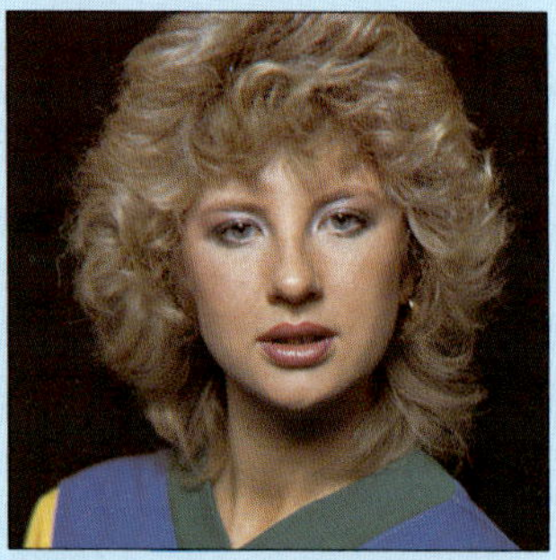
Light close to the lens axis, but raised above the camera.

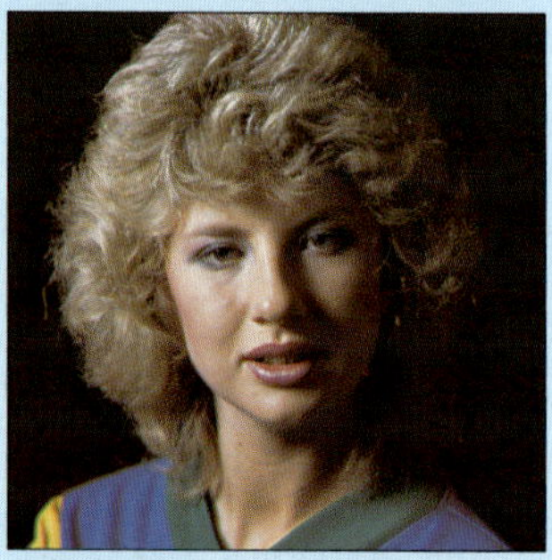
Light at 45° to the lens axis, and angled down at about 45° to the face.

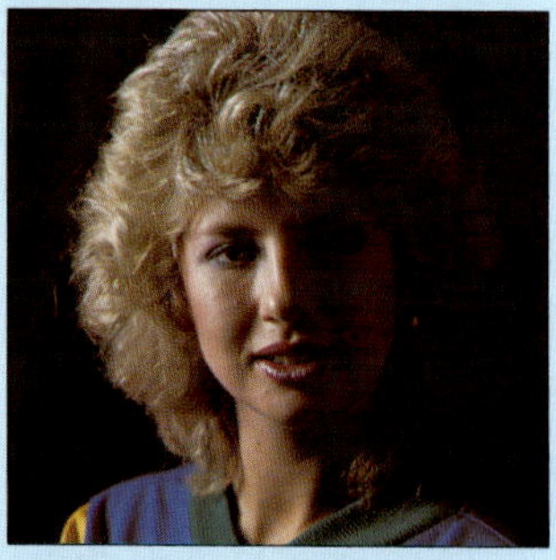
Light at 90° to the lens axis.

Whenever studio photographers are shown at work in films or on television, they are always surrounded by an assortment of studio lights. On large sets, or for special effects, this may be necessary, but not in a small studio. Here, you should try to use as few lights as possible. Partly, this is to save space. Three lighting stands with reflectors and accessories can take over most of the floor, leaving little room for the subject. Mostly, though, you'll find that the best results come from using the minimum number of lights required for a particular effect. Each additional light brings new problems.

In fact, when starting with studio lighting, it is a good idea to spend your first session or two working with just a single light. Almost all lighting set-ups are based on one main light — until you know where and how to position this, you are wasting time and money trying to use two or more lights. If you can only afford one studio flash unit to begin with, don't feel that this puts you at a disadvantage. If you buy two or more together, perhaps as part of a kit, leave the additional units packed away until you can get good results with the first. And if you have been using studio flash for a while, try shooting with just one light at your next session, to see just how much you have learnt so far.

For your initial shots, you can even forget about any reflectors. Try using the flash direct. You will soon discover that lighting is not about light at all — it's about shadows.

You need to work in an area that is fairly dark. Any bright light coming through a window or doorway will swamp the effect of the modelling light. However, you don't need total darkness. Simply closing curtains over a window may be adequate. Use a single subject, rather than a group. Many books on lighting use an egg to show the basic effects, and you could do a lot worse for your first session. Eggs are fairly patient subjects, willing to stay put while you move the light around and study the effect through the camera viewfinder. On the other hand, eggs are probably not going to feature high on your list of future subjects, so a person might offer a more realistic subject for your camera. Be sure to explain that you are carrying out a series of lighting tests, or they may think you are merely incompetent!

Start with the light immediately behind the camera, and as close to camera level as possible — as if you were shooting with a battery flashgun on the camera. Then raise it several feet above camera height, angled down at the subject, and see what an improvement this makes. It looks more natural, because we are use to seeing things lit from above by the sun.

Move the light to the side of the camera, first at 30° and 45°, then at 90°. If you are photographing a person, see how the effect changes when they face the camera, and then when they turn to give a profile to the camera. See what happens to the profile when the light is taken round behind the subject, first at 45°, and then immediately behind the subject, in line with the camera.

The main point of this exercise is not to take prize-winning pictures (though it is possible), but simply to appreciate that a wide range of different effects is at your disposal with just one light.

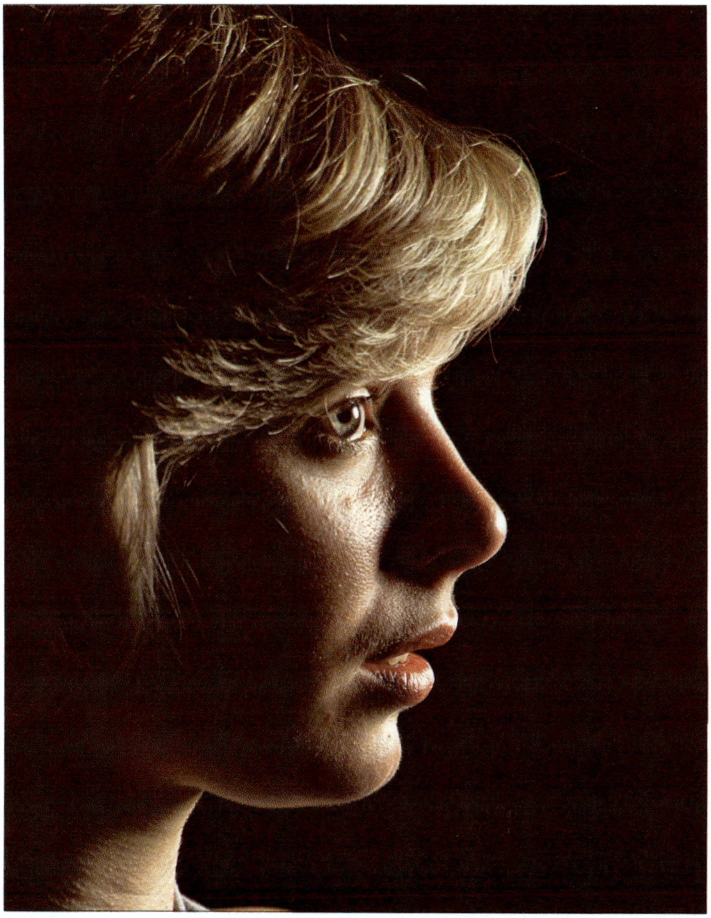

Left: There is no need to feel limited by a single light. It can produce striking effects, even when used without any flash accessories. This profile portrait was taken with the flash unit positioned round to the rear of the girl, and to one side. The light is hitting the face from behind, with the angle carefully chosen so that part of the cheek nearest the camera receives some of the illumination. You need a studio length of about 15 feet for this set-up, but only a narrow width. Any dark background will give a rich black in the picture, since no light falls on it.

Below: The 'spotlight' technique is very effective with many still-life subjects. Here, the flash unit is a few feet above the table-top, positioned slightly forward to give the shadow behind the box. The pool of light is created by fitting a 'snoot' to the flash reflector (see page 36). The background is a sheet of coloured paper. The paper itself has an even tone - it is the pool of light which creates the red and black areas. Red is a dominant colour and will always add impact to your pictures.

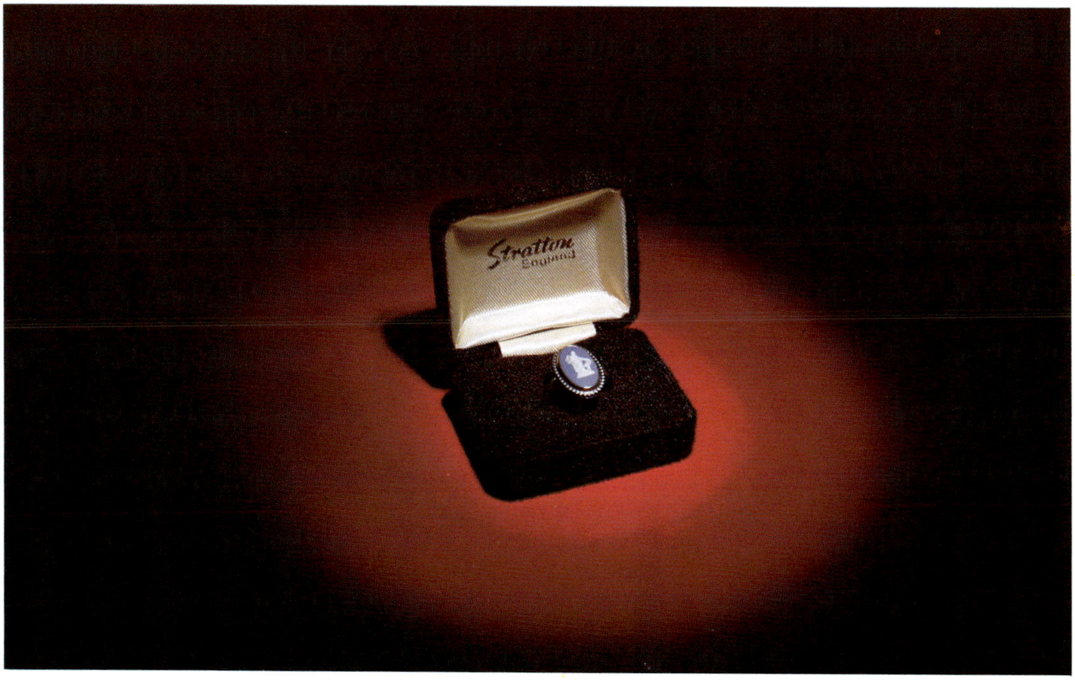

THE BROLLY REFLECTOR

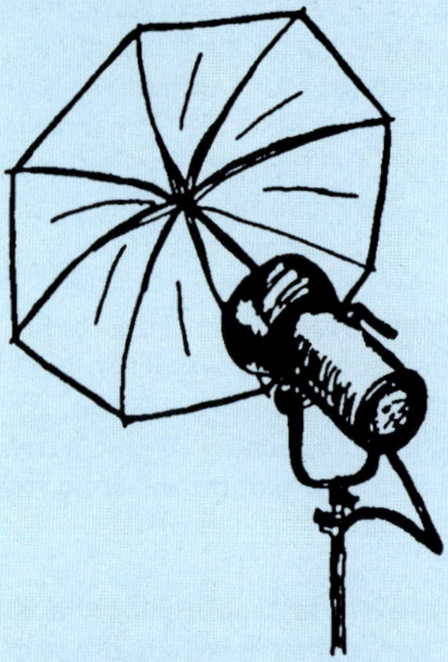

A flash brolly is one of the first accessories you should buy for your studio flash unit. It diffuses the illumination, giving more detail in the highlights and softer shadows. You don't need a brolly for every flash unit — in many set-ups, especially in small studio areas, it is only used on the main unit.

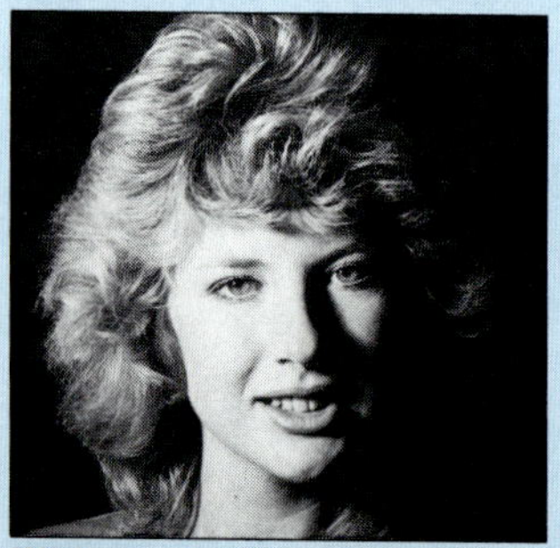

Without a brolly reflector

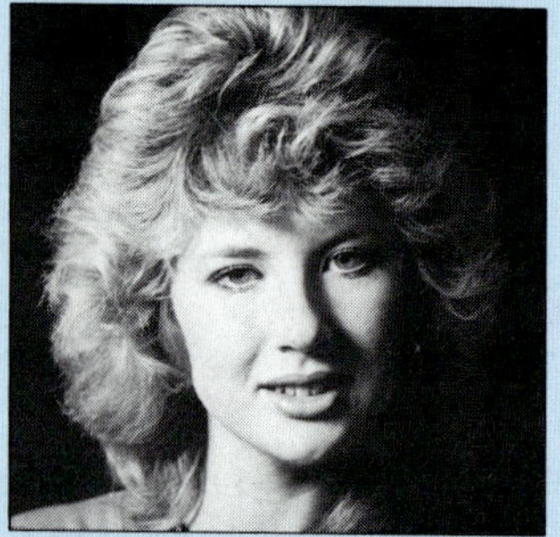

With a brolly reflector

If you have carried out the single light exercise described on the previous page, you will have discovered an overriding characteristic of direct studio flash. It is very contrasty. The highlights are very white, and the shadows are black, with little tone in between. (If you were working in a small room with light-coloured walls, reflections from the walls may have softened the contrast for you.)

The contrast has nothing to do with the fact you are using mains-powered flash. Contrast is controlled by the size of the reflector. That's why small battery-powered flashguns give such a contrasty light. If your studio flash has interchangeable reflectors, you can alter the quality of the light to some extent by fitting the largest. The softest illumination comes from the 'flood' reflector, which uses a suspended metal baffle to prevent direct light from the flash tube reaching the subject.

The flood reflector is perfect for many still-life subjects, but the illumination it provides can still be too contrasty for portraits. The 'brolly' reflector is usually better, and it can be used with every type and model of studio flash. As the name suggests, it is made of a reflective material, rather than metal, and opens out on a spine frame, just like an umbrella. When collapsed, it packs away into a small space — ideal for the home studio photographer.

The central shaft of the open brolly reflector is a metal rod. This slides down a central metal tube in the flash unit, and is locked into place by a retaining screw. It is important not to push the brolly shaft too far into the flash unit. If the reflector surface is too close to the flash, only the central area will receive light. The softest illumination comes from using the entire area of the surface. You can usually tell by looking into the reflector whether or not all of the surface is being illuminated. As a general rule, the shaft of the brolly should extend to the end of the flash unit, but not beyond it.

There are several types of flash brolly available. First, there is a choice of size. The larger the reflector, the softer the light. However, the larger sizes can be difficult to manoeuvre in confined areas, so the small brolly is often better to begin with. If you find you can handle this with room to spare, put a larger brolly on your shopping list.

Brollies also come with nylon or metallic finishes, and with a choice of silver or gold in the latter. White nylon gives the softest light, and can be used as a reflector or a diffuser. It's not very efficient as a reflector, since a lot of light passes through. The double nylon brolly cuts down on this light loss. For greater efficiency, though with a slight increase in contrast, use a metallic reflector. No light passes through this, and although there is some absorption, you'll find that a metallic reflector generally allows you to work at an aperture one stop smaller than an equivalent nylon reflector.

A gold reflector adds warmth to colour images and is particularly good for portraits. Silver is a good general purpose reflector and is probably the best first choice. When using a silver brolly, you can create the warmth of a gold reflector by using an 81A or 81B filter (or equivalent) to the camera lens. Larger brollies are often reversible, giving the choice between a metallic finish and white.

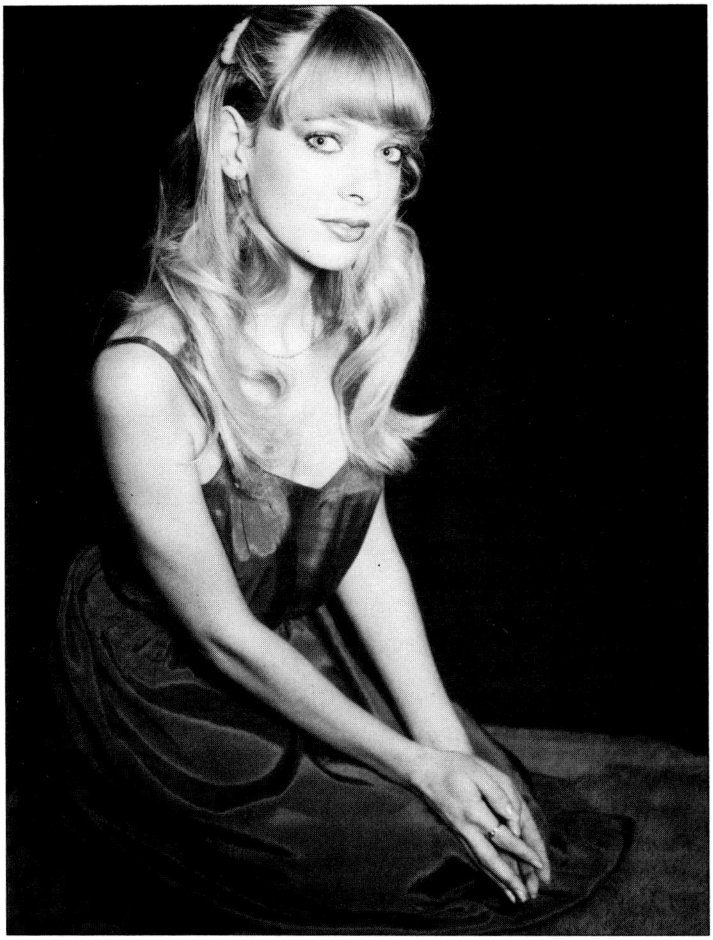

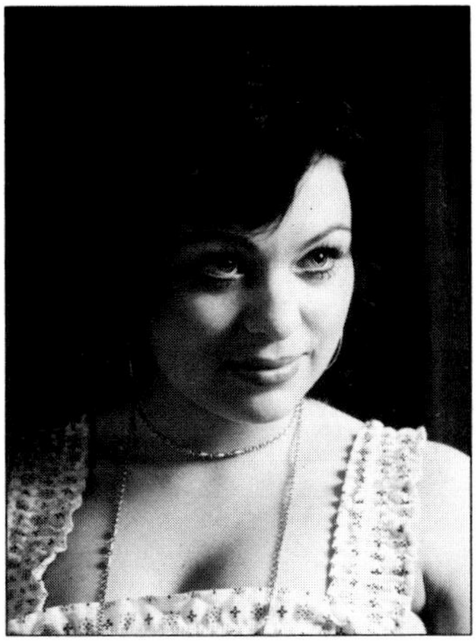

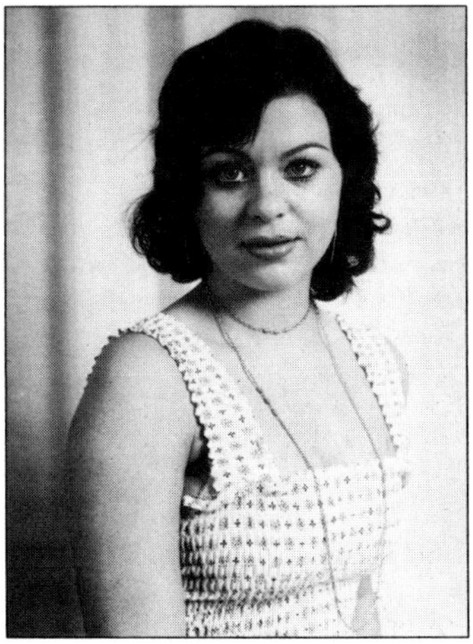

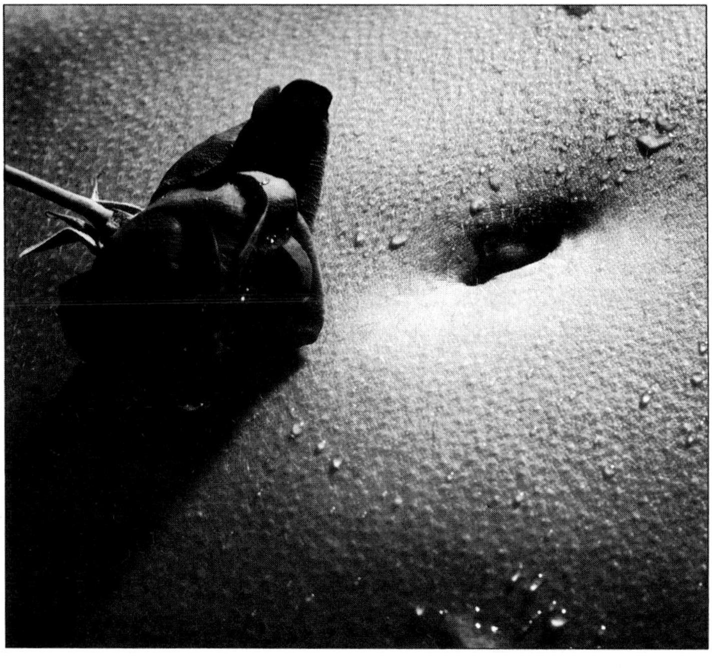

Above: A single light with brolly reflector can be used to produce a variety of effects. With portraits, for example, simply altering the colour of the background, and the distance between the subject and the camera, can give very different results. The two small pictures *(above top and bottom)* use dark and light plain backgrounds fairly close to the subject. The larger portrait *(above left)* is taken in an ordinary living room. The background is dark because the girl has been positioned in the centre of the room, away from furniture and walls.

Left: This low key image was produced by positioning the flash unit and brolly behind and above the subject. The shadows are being thrown forward.

USING A SHEET REFLECTOR

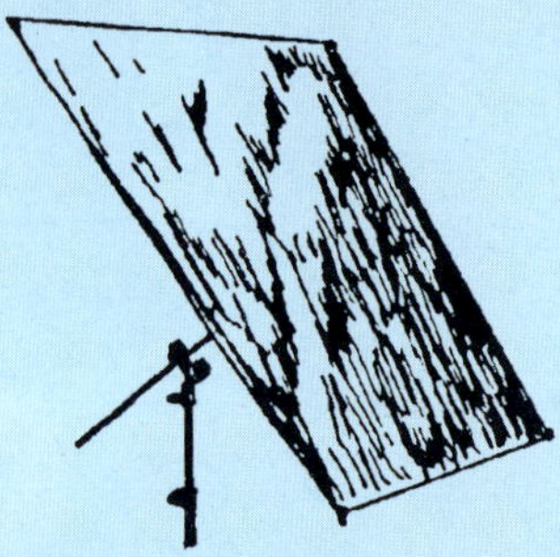

Almost any type of light-toned material can be used as a reflector. A white sheet hanging from a clothes dryer may be all you need! However, a specially designed photographic reflector, such as the Courtenay Variflecta, offers many advantages. It has a reversible metallic and white surface, folds away into a small space, can be raised and lowered on its stand, will also tilt. This last feature is extremely useful, since it allows you to reflect light to the underside of your subject.

Safety note
Photo reflector sheets are often supported by a frame which has a long tubular shaft. This can be at eye height in the studio, and is difficult to see in the dim light. Push a cork onto the end of the shaft to prevent any accidents.

Even with a large brolly reflector, you may find that the illumination is still too contrasty. Unless the light is used square on to the subject, the shadows will probably lack detail. Many lighting books recommend the use of a second flash unit, positioned close to the camera, to add light to these dark areas. This is wasteful. There are much better things to do with a second unit than fill-in the shadow areas. Also, a second light used near the camera creates the problem of a second set of shadows, and can add an extra set of catchlights to a portrait.

A simple sheet reflector will add all the detail you need to the shadows, and avoids any of the problems of the fill-in light. A sheet reflector can be a length of white cloth hung from a frame, a piece of polystyrene, a sheet of white-painted hardboard, or a purpose-designed photographic reflector. The photo reflector will usually be the most versatile, with a frame that can be tilted as well as raised and lowered. Photo reflectors are available in a range of surfaces, generally matching the surfaces available for brolly reflectors. Like the larger brolly reflectors, the sheet reflector is often reversible.

Positioning the sheet reflector is simple. It goes on the opposite side of the subject to the studio flash unit, so that it can pick up the light and bounce it back.

The sheet reflector gives you a lot of control over the light. Use a metallic reflector close to the subject and the shadows will virtually disappear. Move the reflector back and the shadows will appear, but with plenty of detail. If you can't move the reflector back far enough in a small studio area, use a white surface and less light will be added to the subject.

To judge the effect of the reflector, stand by the camera and look at the subject through half-closed eyes. This will give you an approximate idea of the tonal range that will be seen by the photographic film. Your eyes are much more sensitive than film in low light, and accommodate a much greater brightness range, so don't assume that all the detail you can see in the subject will be recorded.

Sheet reflectors are ideal for portraiture and other subjects of similar size, but they are too large and awkward for small table-top sets. Here, the ideal reflectors are the white polystyrene blocks that are used to pack and protect a wide range of products. Sometimes you'll come across quite large sheets of the material, but mostly they are moulded blocks. These blocks are particularly good for small subjects because you can place the polystyrene next to the subject without additional support. Two or three of the blocks can be arranged round the subject to bring out the full shadow detail. Next time you come across suitable pieces of polystyrene, store them in your studio cupboard and try them out during the next session.

Aluminium foil stretched over a sheet of card also makes a good customised reflector. Use the shiny side out for the strongest effect, the dull side for a weaker fill-in. The smooth foil may give 'hot-spots' if it reflects a direct image of the flash into the subject. Crumpling the foil before smoothing it over the card will give a more diffuse reflection.

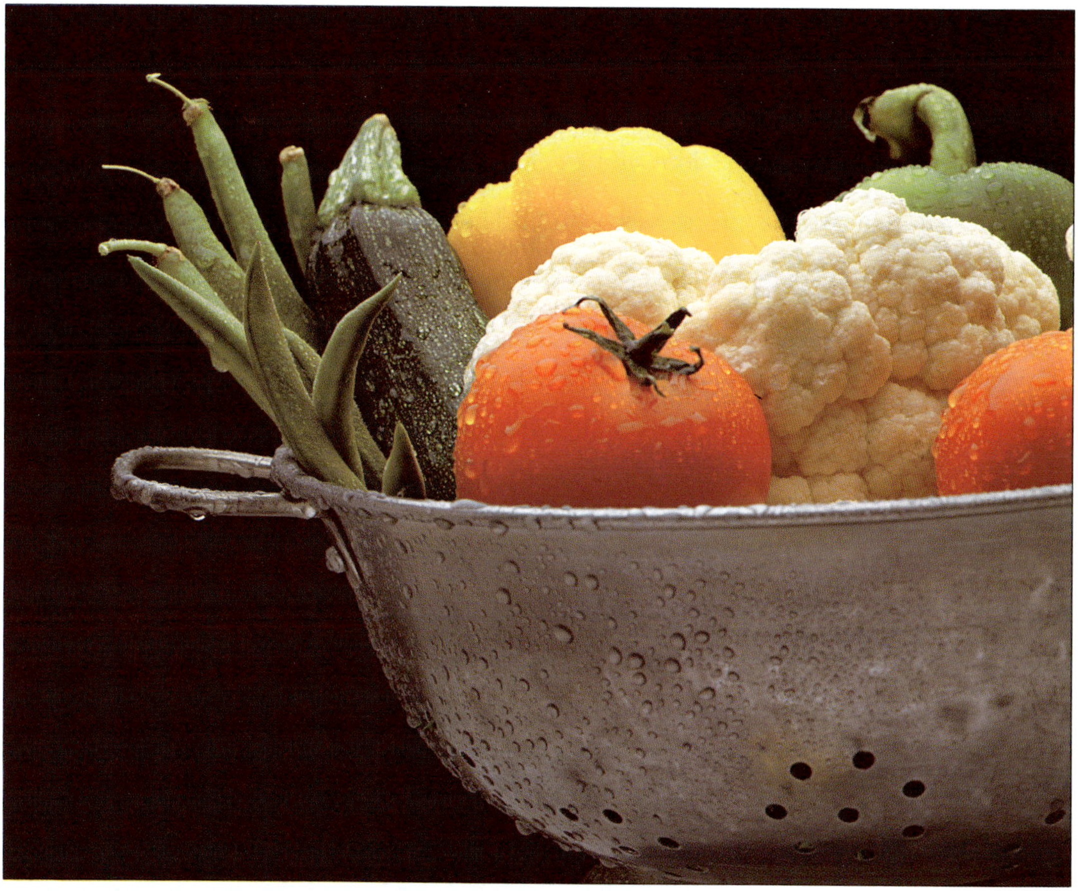

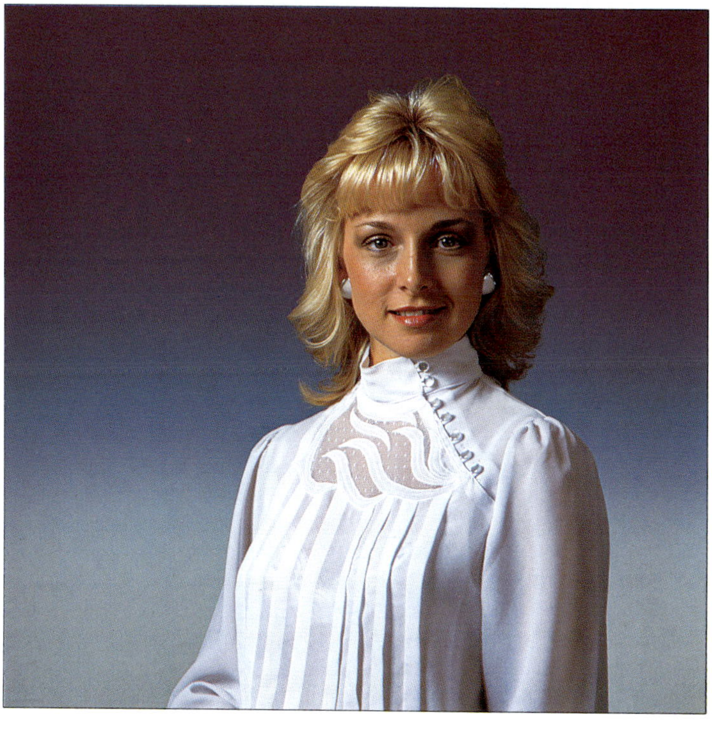

Above: The main light for these fresh vegetables is overhead, shining down on the subject. A white reflector positioned in front of the set-up, below camera height, adds detail to the aluminium container.

Left: Effective portraits can be taken with just a single light (on the left of the camera) and a reflector (on the right of the camera. **Below**: The same set-up taken without the reflector.

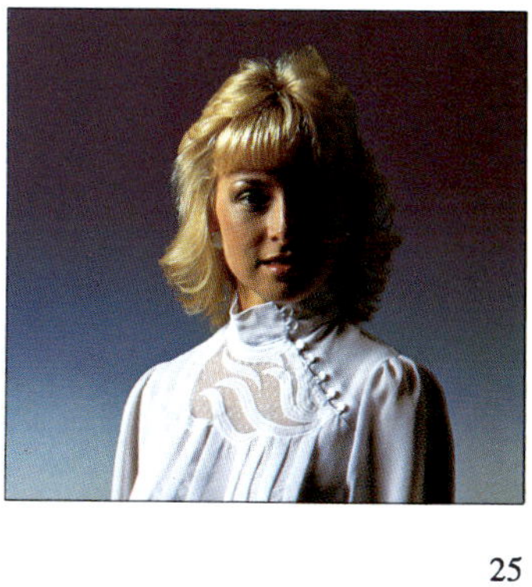

USING DIFFUSERS

A white nylon brolly acts as a diffuser when turned around so that light from the flash unit passes through to the subject. However, there is considerable loss of light, since much of the illumination is reflected back to the flash unit. More efficient is the Courtenay Varifuser Assembly. This is a simple frame which supports a large square sheet of diffuser material. Three different sheets are supplied with the outfit, giving different degrees of diffusion. The diffuser material is thinner than the white nylon used for brolly reflectors, so more light reaches the subject. The most effective diffuser for the small studio is the Courtenay Windolite. This unit packs into a very small space, but opens out to produce an accessory which clips onto the flash reflector (below). A big advantage is that light reflected back from the

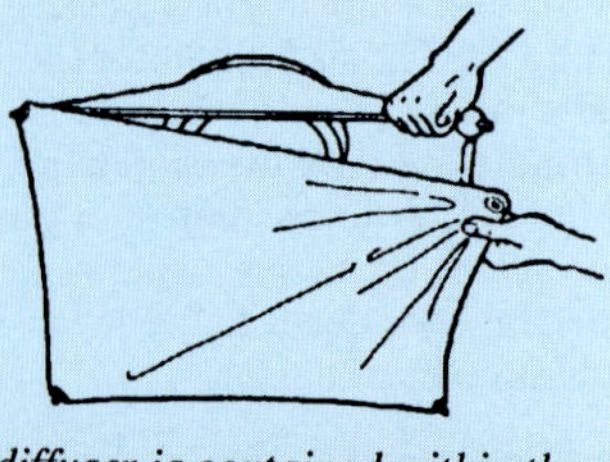

diffuser is contained within the unit and does not bounce around the studio. The Windolite is particularly good for still-life photography, though it also gives good results with portraits and other subjects.

The high contrast lighting from a studio flash unit can be softened by a diffuser. This is usually positioned about a foot in front of the flash reflector. As with the brolly reflector, the diffuser turns the small source of light into a larger area of light, and it is this which reduces the contrast of the illumination. If the diffuser is placed too close to the flash unit, the overall effect will be negligible.

You can make your own diffuser. All you need is a length of net curtain, or a thin sheet of white cloth, hung from a support in front of the flash. However, in the confined space of a home studio, a diffuser sold as an accessory for the flash unit will probably be more convenient, since it will not need a separate stand. Some systems are supplied with a selection of diffuser materials so that you can select the degree of softness required. This type of accessory is most useful for table-top photography. For general use, and particularly for portrait photography, a white nylon brolly is quite effective. Instead of bouncing the light from the inside surface on to the subject, turn the assembly round so that light passing through the brolly reaches the subject. The brolly, of course, is still acting as a reflector as well, so quite a lot of the light is being wasted. Even worse, it is being reflected into the studio and can alter the overall lighting effect, or even cause flare in the camera lens. A more efficient accessory consists of an enclosed frame which stretches a sheet of white nylon in front of the flash reflector. This is usually called a 'window light' (or some variation of these words) because the illumination provided is similar to daylight coming through a window. Bigger is better when it comes to any form of diffuser. If you have choice, go for the largest size that can be used conveniently in your studio space.

A studio flash unit fitted with a small or medium-size window light is likely to be more manageable than the unit fitted with a brolly reflector. This makes it much more suitable for overhead lighting, particularly for table-top photography. It is not so effective for backlighting, since it is more difficult to shield the large bright surface from the camera lens and this increases the risk of flare.

Diffused illumination is good for high-key lighting effects, but only if you use the flash unit close to the camera, or have two window lights, one on either side of the camera. A window light used on its own is, in fact, excellent for low-key lighting, since the highlight and shadows created have very soft edges. And a diffused light source used with a separate reflector is very versatile. In a small studio area, a small window light and an adjustable reflector takes up less space than most other set-ups, but can be used for a wide range of effects.

However, don't expect too much from a window light in your home studio. The chances are that the diffuser area will be relatively small, and the softening effect on the illumination may not be much more than that provided by a brolly reflector. Professional studios use window lights which are four feet square, or larger. The only way you can produce similar effects from small diffusers is to use two or more units side by side. Alternatively, you can build a large wooden frame and stretch diffuser material across it. Position the frame in your set and aim two or more flash units through the material.

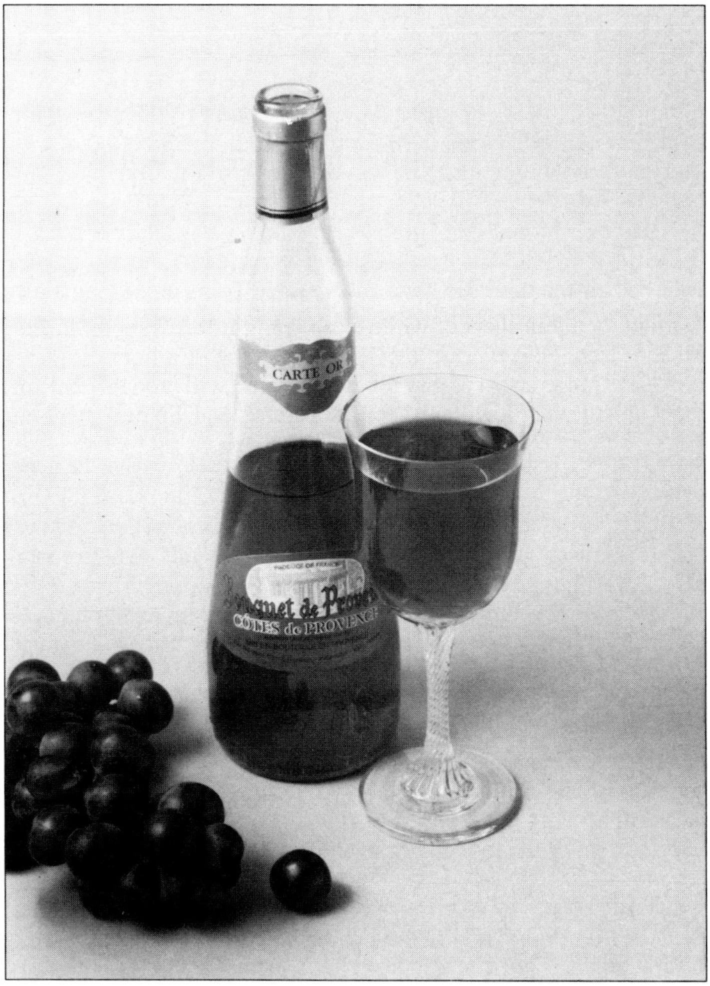

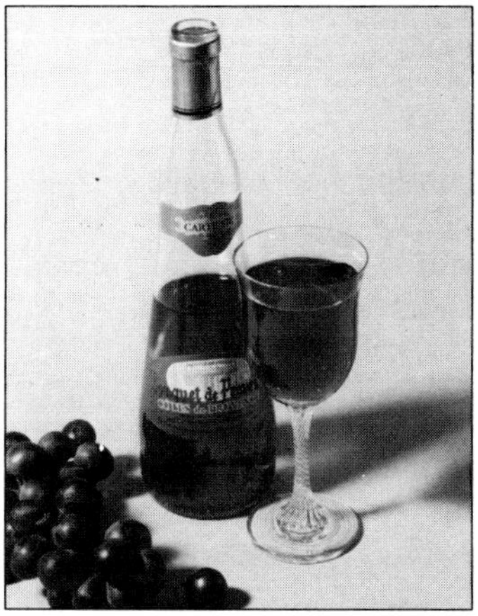

Left: A simple still-life set-up shot using a heavy diffuser in front of the flash reflector. **Above**: The same set-up without the diffuser. Notice the heavier shadows thrown across the surface of the table. The degree of diffusion can be controlled both by the type of diffuser material used, and the distance of the diffuser from the flash reflector. The greater the distance, the greater the diffusion.

Below: The soft highlight shadow in this shot was created by a 'window light' diffuser in front of the flash. The light is positioned high above the subject, and slightly to the rear. The background was lit separately.

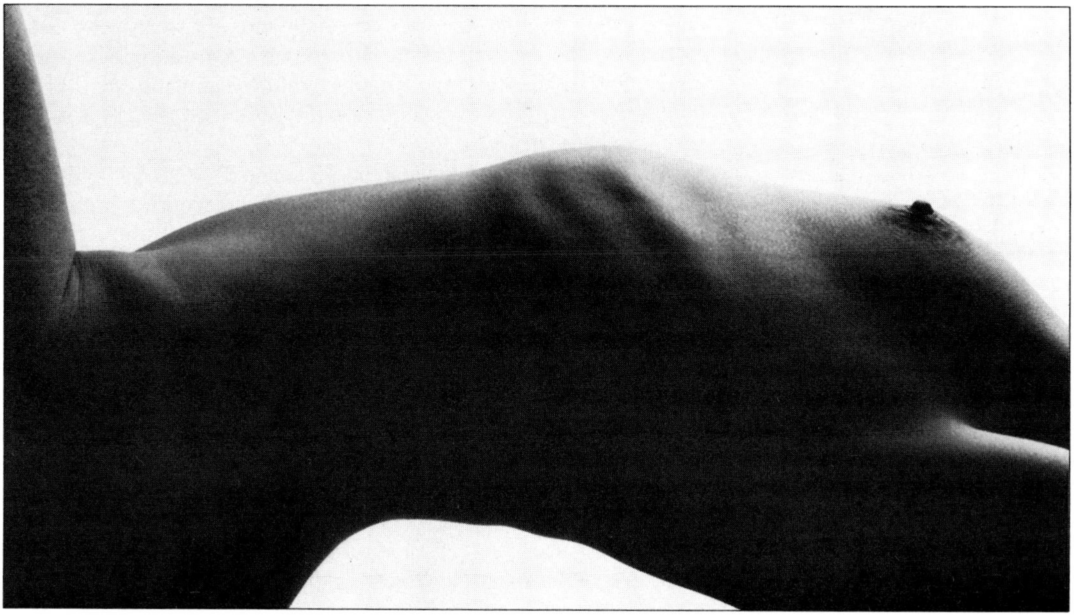

ADDING A SECOND LIGHT

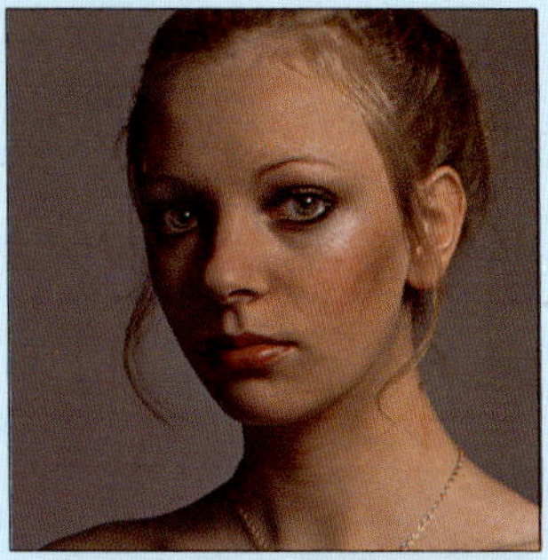

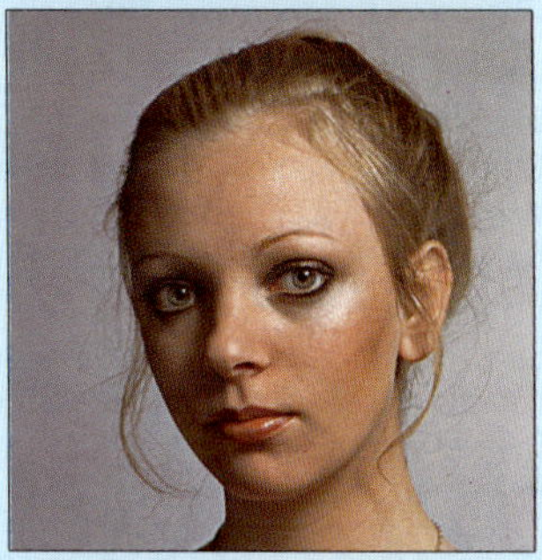

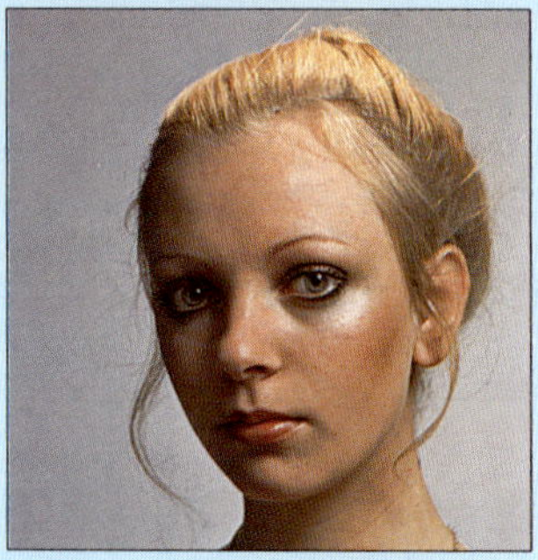

***Above**: Adding a background light (centre) and a hair light (bottom) creates a different image to just the main light (top). There is more information on how to use additional lights on the following pages.*

Opposite: Most studio portraits and glamour shots you see in magazines will have been taken with more than one light. The additional lights are often used to backlight the hair, or to illuminate the background. This has the effect of separating the subject from the background, giving the impression of depth to the image.

Although excellent photographs can be produced using a single flash unit and reflectors, the set-up has its limitations. Sooner or later, and probably sooner, you will want to start experimenting with a second light.

Adding a second light is relatively simple, especially if it has a built-in slave cell. As soon as it is connected to the mains and switched on, the slave cell should react to the firing of the main flash unit and fire its own flash at the same moment. In small studio sets, it is extremely rare for the slave cell to be in a position where it cannot pick up the main flash — the cell is usually sufficiently sensitive to work from reflected light, even if it is not in a direct line with the main flash. However, to be on the safe side, it is worth test firing the main flash and checking that the second flash fires. This is the main purpose of the test button on the control panel of the flash unit.

It is possible to check that the second flash fires by looking into the reflector as your press the test button, but this is not recommended. Although the bright flash is unlikely to do any harm to your eyes, it will prevent you from seeing clearly for up to a minute, or more. This won't help the accuracy of your focusing. It's much better to concentrate on a point several feet to one side of the reflector as you press the test button. Your peripheral vision will see the flash quite clearly without affecting your vision.

If the control panel of the second unit is facing you, check the test by watching the small neon light which blinks rapidly to indicate that the flash is ready for firing. If the neon goes out for a second or so after you press the test button of the main flash, it shows that the second unit has fired and is recycling. Bright daylight can reduce the sensitivity of the slave cell to the point where it will not react to the main flash. If you can't cut out the daylight, or are using the studio flash with daylight, you will have to connect the two flash units by a synchronizing cable. This is a lead with a large jack plug at either end. It plugs into the spare socket on the main flash unit and either of the sockets on the second unit. In effect, both units are now connected to the camera synchronization lead and should fire together. It's still worth pressing the test button on one unit to make sure the other fires.

A synchronization cable can also be used if the second unit does not have a built-in slave. However, it is good working practice to avoid unnecessary trailing leads in a small, dimly lit studio area, so it's much better to buy a plug in slave cell. If you can't find a slave cell with the jack plug fitting, buy a slave unit designed for battery flashguns, plus a camera synchronization cable with jack plug at one end and 3mm co-axial socket at the other. Connect the slave cell to the flash unit via the cable (a hot-shoe adaptor may also be needed with some slave cells). It's a good idea to fix the slave to the top of the flash unit and tie the spare cable out of the way. However, the slave and cable could be trailed along a wall or floor to give better sight of the main flash — a useful technique for those occasions when the slave cell of the second unit is hidden from view and you don't want to use a synchronization cable. You can use as many slave cells, or synchronization cables, as there are additional lights.

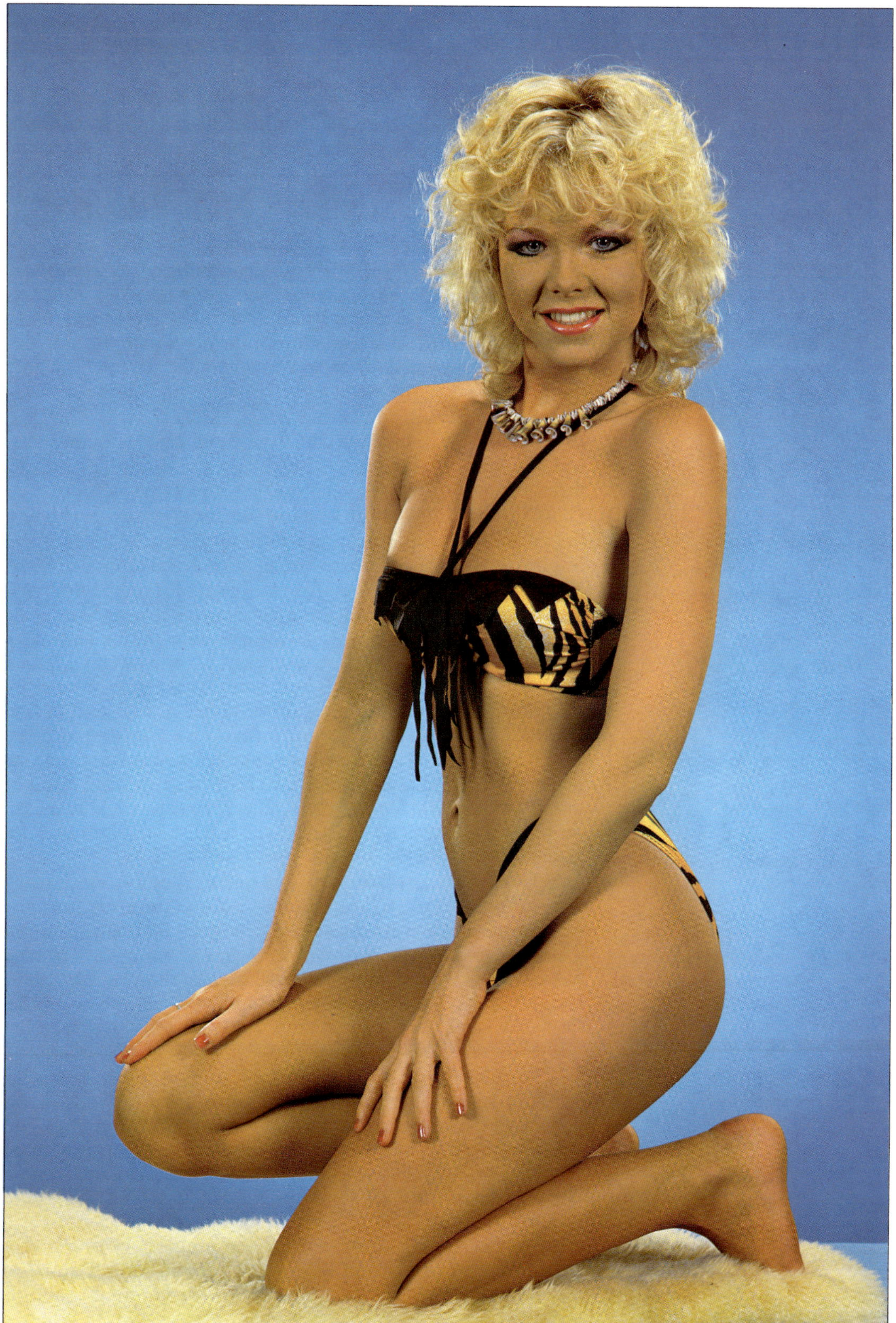

STUDIO FLASH EXPOSURE

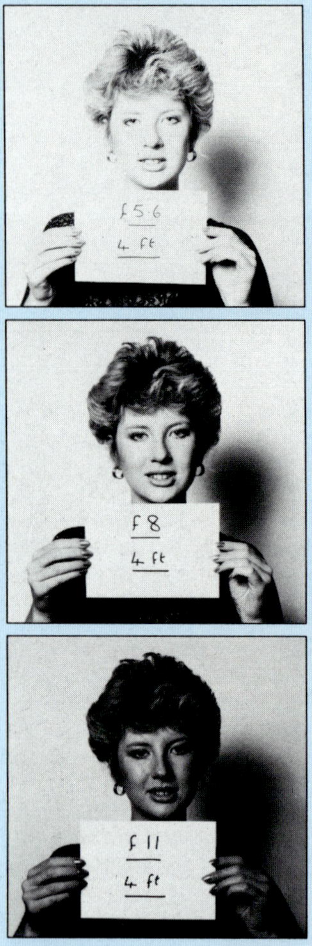

When shooting your series of test exposures, it's a good idea to write the aperture and flash distance for each exposure in thick felt-tip pen on a sheet of paper and include this information in the frame. Then, when you come to examine the processed film, you won't make a mistake in deciding which aperture gives the best exposure. Only three examples are reproduced here, with f/8 showing the correct exposure. Normally, you would shoot a series of six test frames, at apertures from f/2.8 to f/16.

Photographers with the latest auto-everything cameras are sometimes shocked to discover that they have to switch their camera to full manual control for studio flash photography. Program and automatic metering modes are not effective with flash. Even those cameras with through-the-lens flash metering only give this facility with special dedicated units. With studio flash, the camera shutter speed and aperture must be set manually.

The shutter speed is set to the synchronization speed *(see page 18)* and remains fixed throughout the studio session. Flash exposure is controlled only by the lens aperture. And since many of your home studio lighting set-ups will be very similar, the lens aperture is also likely to remain much the same throughout the session. The only problem is finding the correct aperture in the first place.

A flash meter will provide the answer *(see next page)*. But if you have just a single studio flash unit, there are other more useful accessories to spend your money on. Shooting a test film will give all the exposure information you need, and costs a lot less money.

All you need do is set up a typical subject. Portraits are good for test films, since exposure errors show up clearly in the face and features. Find a patient person and sit them in a comfortable chair. Position your camera at least four feet away. Set up the flash unit (and reflector, if used) about three feet from the subject, at an angle of about 45° to the camera. Load the camera with film and take a series of exposures at aperture settings of f/2.8, f/4, f/5.6, f/8, f/11 and f/16. Transparency film is best, since it has the least exposure latitude and will show correct exposures quite clearly. Negative film is satisfactory if you can judge correct exposure from the processed film. Don't rely on prints, since quite acceptable prints can be obtained from negatives which have been overexposed by two or three stops. ISO 100 film is a good choice for most home studio flash set-ups. Faster film can be used if you need smaller apertures for greater depth-of-field.

When you have completed the first run of exposures, measure the distance between the subject and the flash unit (measure from any point on the unit, but always use the same point for future measurements). Then move the flash further away and repeat the same run of exposures. Finally, move the flash even further way and take a final six shots. Make sure you measure the distance between the flash unit and the subject each time. The entire test can be taken on a 20-exposure film.

When the film is processed, study each series of exposures carefully and make a note of the aperture used for each of the correctly exposed frames. Write this on a small label and attach it to the side of the flash unit. Now, when you come to take further studio flash pictures, all you have to do is measure the distance between the unit and the subject and set the appropriate aperture. The use of different reflectors will affect the exposure, but another test will soon set this right. Once you have a basic setting, you can do other tests at the end of a studio session, so that you don't have to set everything up specially each time. You'll be surprised how little aperture adjustment is needed between different types of set-up.

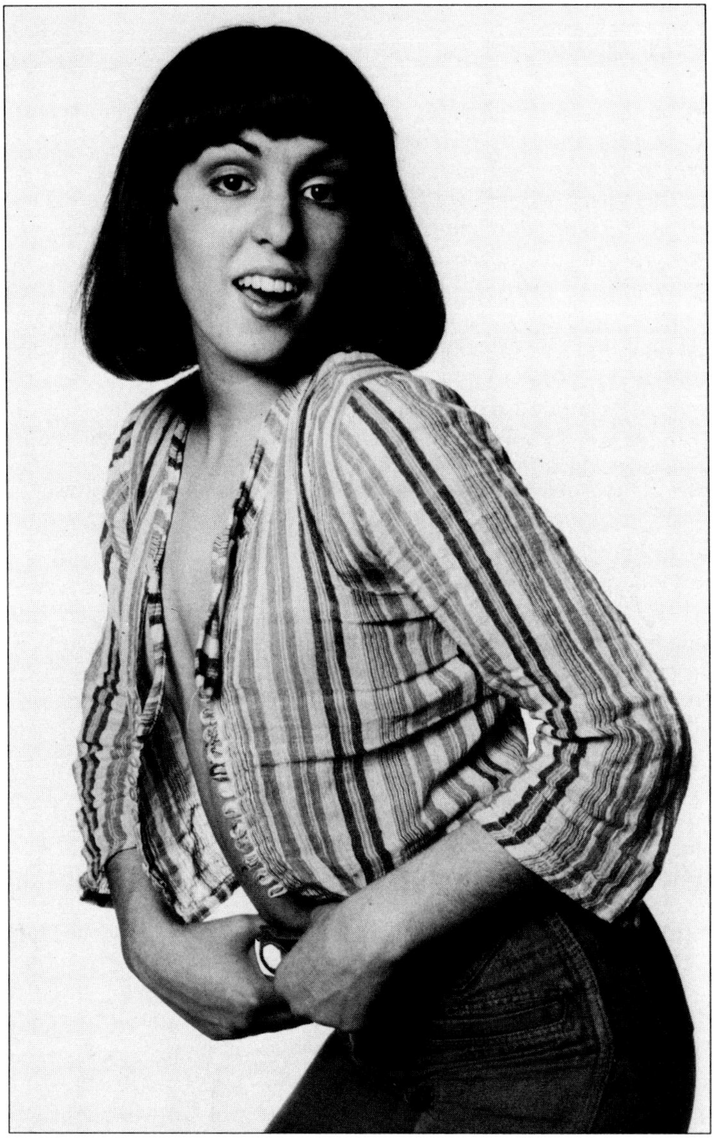

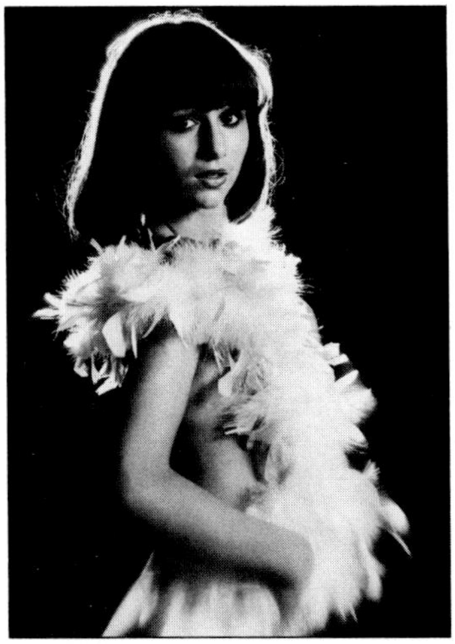

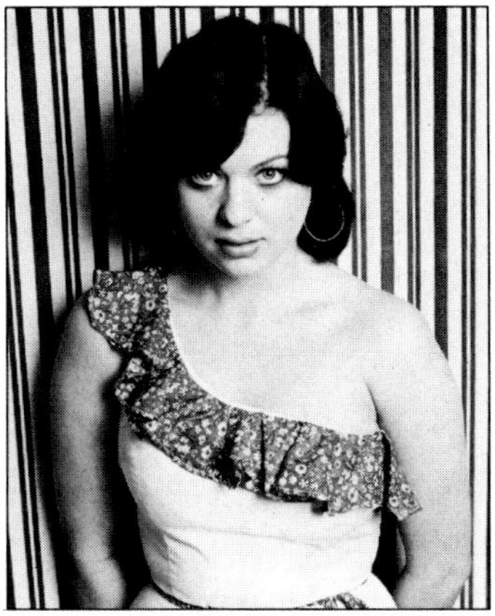

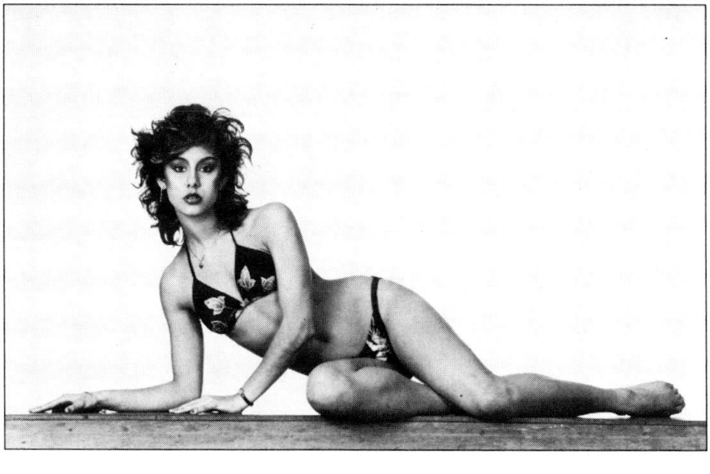

These four pictures, although they appear quite different, all have one thing in common. They were all taken at a lens aperture of f/8. In fact, the majority of black-and-white pictures in this book were taken at f/8, since the main light used for all of them was a Courtenay Solaflash 1000 (or the earlier Colorflash units) and the film was always Ilford FP4. Using the same main light in similar conditions generally means that the main exposure will stay constant. Changes in background or the use of additional lights, has little effect on the main exposure. The main exception to this rule comes when you move in close to your subject, perhaps filling the frame with just the face of a portrait subject. Here, because of the increased extension between lens and film, you need to give up to one stop extra exposure.

EXPOSURE METERING

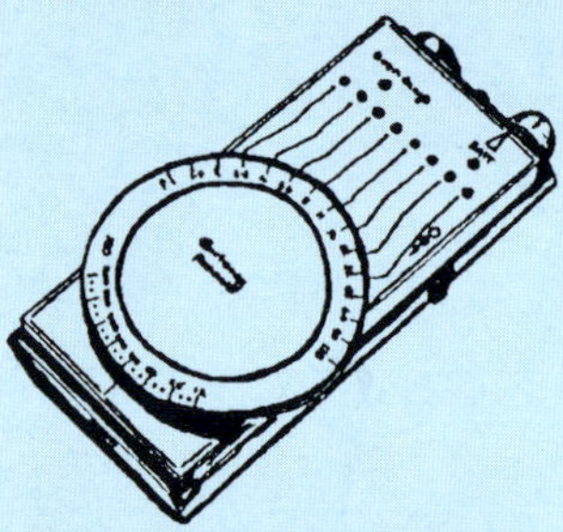

The Courtenay Flash Meter is a versatile accessory which will cover all your small studio requirements. It can be used with or without direct connection to the flash units, and for incident or reflected light readings. Once the film speed has been set, a series of red light-emitting diodes indicate the recommended lens aperture to the nearest half-stop.

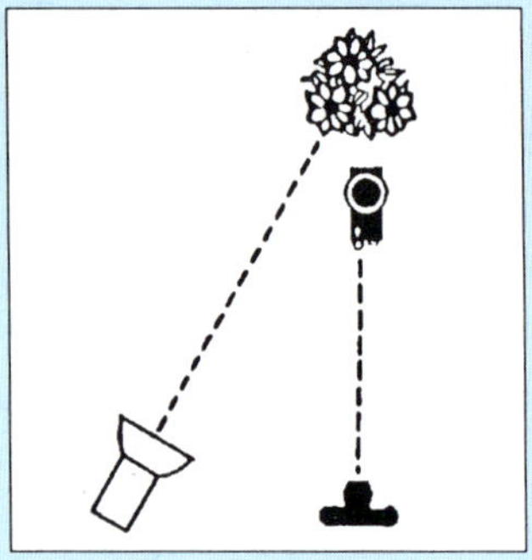

An incident light reading measures the light reaching the subject.

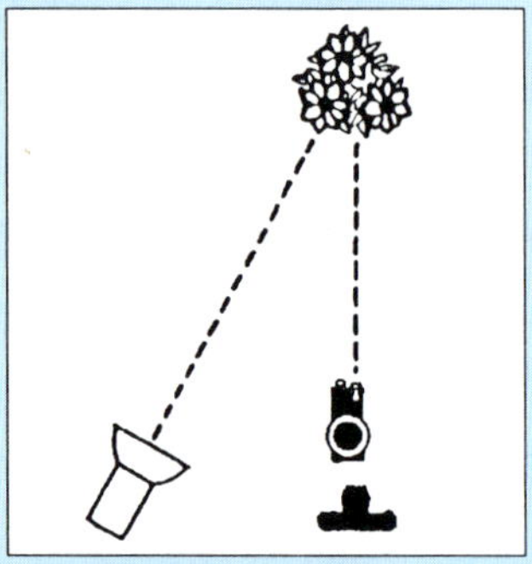

A reflected light reading measures the light reflected from the subject. Not recommended for studio flash.

When just a single flash unit is being used, a test film will pinpoint the best lens aperture for correct exposure. This aperture will not need to be altered very much unless there is a major change to the lighting set-up. Adding a reflector should not alter the exposure. The reflector is only adding light to the shadow areas, it is not affecting the highlights in any way.

Even when additional flash units are used, you should find that the main exposure remains much the same. There ought to be only one main light — the additional lights are not usually aimed at the front of the subject.

So why do you need a flash meter? The answer is that you don't — but you will find one very useful, particularly for multiple flash set-ups. A flash meter can allow fine adjustments to the aperture setting, especially if you are using studio flash in a range of different locations. But even more useful is the ability of the meter to give you the brightness ratio between different units in a single set.

Flash meters measure incident light. This means that you measure the light falling onto the subject, not the light reflected. The meter instructions will probably tell you to hold the meter alongside the subject and point the measuring cell at the camera. In practice, you might find it better to point the cell at the main light. Check that the meter is set correctly according to the instructions, and then reach out and fire the main flash by pressing the test button on the back of the unit. In a small studio set-up, you are almost certain to be within arm's length of the control panel. If not, and you are taking a portrait, ask your subject to hold the flash while you press the test button. For still-life subjects, you can connect a cable between the flash and the meter, firing a test by pressing a button on the meter. Use a cable as a last resort — the fewer wires trailing about your studio the better.

When you have taken a reading towards the main light, keep the meter alongside the subject, but turn it towards one of the additional lights and take another reading. In small studio areas, there is a good chance the the additional flash units will be used fairly close to the subject, and often without a brolly reflector. This means that the light they give will be probably be much brighter than the main light and the flash meter will indicate a small aperture. You need to reduce the power of the additional lights until you get similar readings from the main light and any additional lights.

If the additional units have a power setting switch, this should be turned lower. If the reading is still too high, see if the light can be moved further from the subject. If not, can the main light be moved closer to allow a smaller aperture? If neither option is possible, you will have to fit a filter holder to each of the additional lights and attach neutral density filters. These reduce the power of the light without affecting the colour.

If you have a flash meter, it is worth taking readings from all the lights every time you move their positions. Additional lights can make a major difference to your photographs, but only if they are correctly balanced with the main light. Remember that the flash meter is not reading through-the-lens. Compensation will be needed if you are using lens filters or converters.

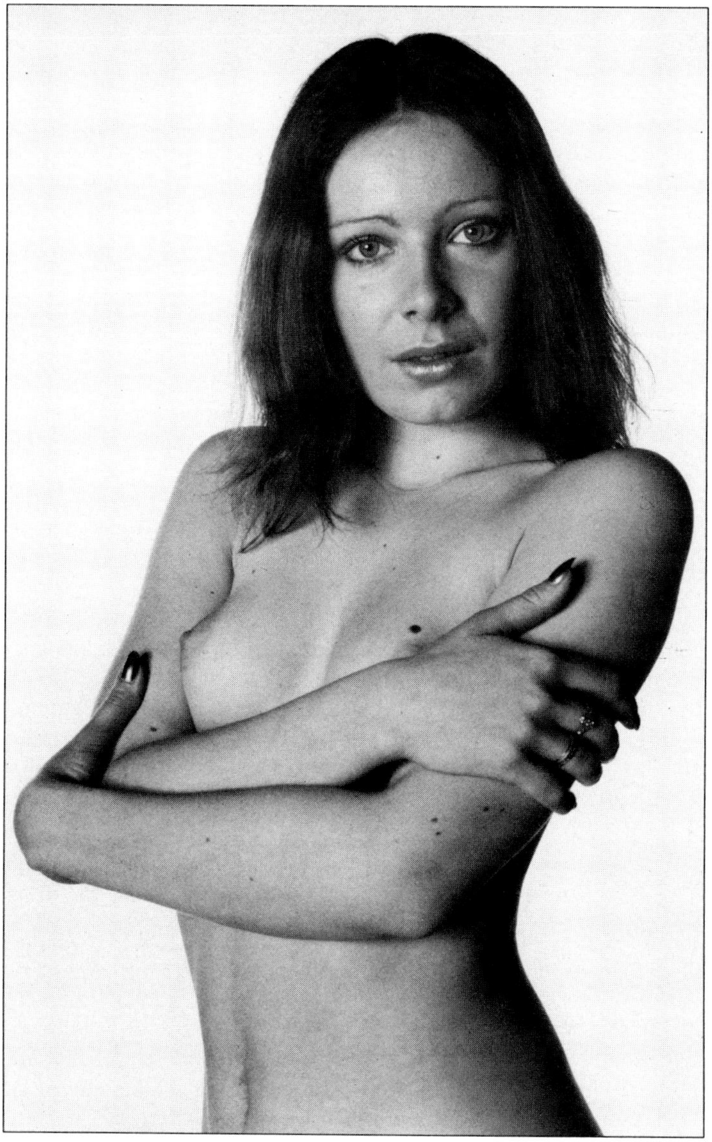

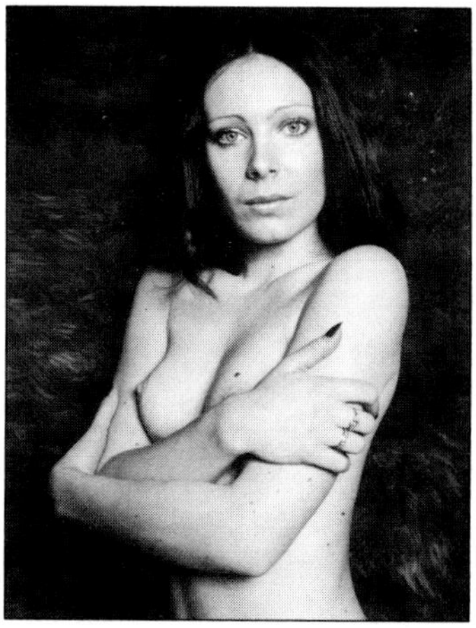

The built-in exposure meter of your camera takes reflected light readings. This simply means that the meter measures the brightness of the light reflected from the subject. For studio flash metering, an incident light meter reading is usually much better. This measures the brightness of the light falling on the subject. Take a look at these two images *(left and above)*. The main subject is the same, with similar lighting. An incident light reading will give the same correct aperture for both, since the meter will see the same brightness of light in each case. A reflected light reading, however, will be influenced by the bright background in one shot and the dark background in the other. Two different apertures will be given, neither of which will be an accurate reading for the main subject.

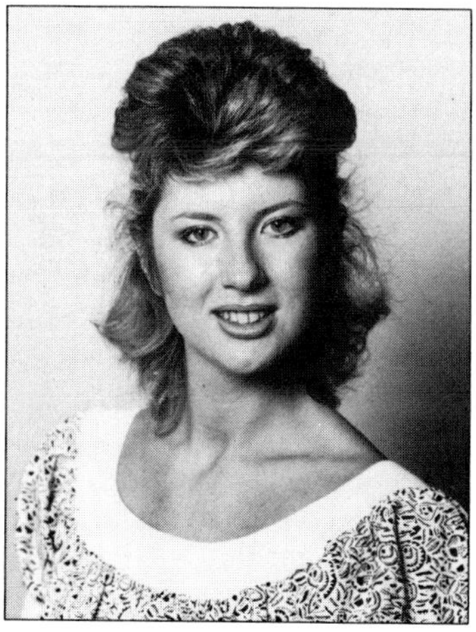

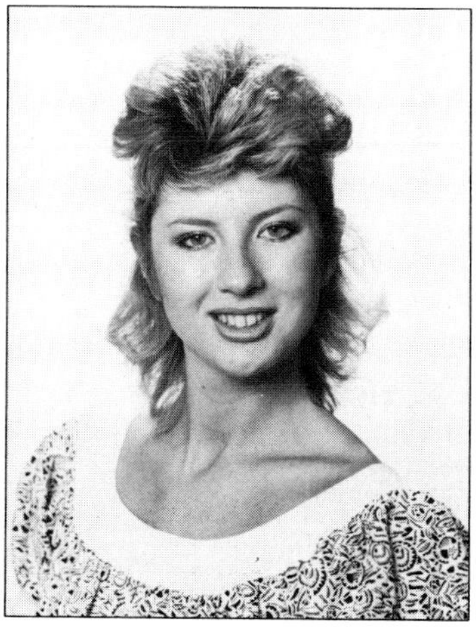

If the picture on the left was shot at an aperture of f/8, what aperture was used for the picture on the right? The answer is f/8. You should not need to alter the aperture when additional lights are added, as long as the light on the subject remains the same. If the additional lights are too bright or too weak, you must alter their distance from the subject, or use filters over the flash heads. If you alter the aperture to suit the additional lights, the exposure for your main subject will be incorrect.

THE MAIN LIGHT

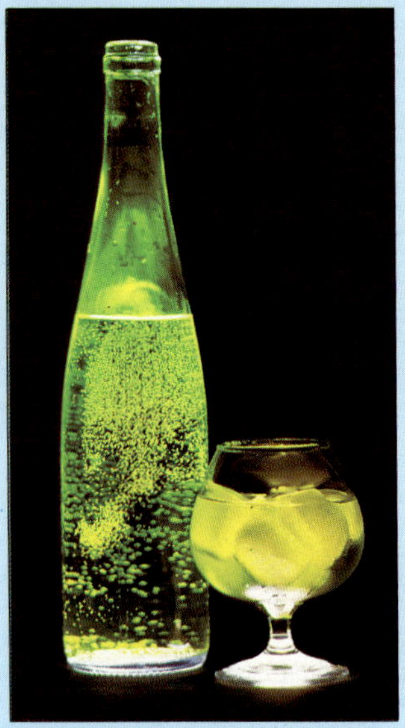

Don't be afraid to experiment with unusual positions for your main light. Here, the bottle and glass are resting on a sheet of plate glass which has been covered with a length of black paper. Two circles have been cut out of the paper and the bottle and glass placed over these holes. The single light is under the work top, shining directly upwards through the plate glass and the subject.

Left: The main light creates the mood of your picture — low-key or high-key, romantic or dramatic. This light should always be positioned first, with all other lights switched off. Sometimes, the main light will be all you need. But often you will want to use additional lights on the background, or for backlighting. These additional lights should always remain subordinate to the main light — they should add the the effect created by the main light, never detract from it.

Home studio lighting sets should be kept as simple as possible. A single main light will be all you need for most subjects. The type of illumination used will vary with the subject. You may want the contrasty light of direct flash, the softer effect of light bounced from a brolly, or the diffused quality of light transmitted through white nylon. But whatever the effect, there are just a few basic positions for the main light — square on to the subject, at right angles to the camera or behind the subject, and somewhere between these extremes. This may sound rather restricting, but it's not. Variations in height and angle allow you to adjust the lighting to suit each individual subject. And there are unusual examples of these positions to consider — shining the light from immediately over the subject, or from underneath, for example.

At first sight, square-on lighting appears the least attractive. After all, flashguns attached to camera are in this position, and the results they give are often flat and lifeless. But camera flashguns are also very close to the lens axis, so the shadows they throw are not seen by the camera. As soon as you start to raise the light above the camera, the downward shadows that appear bring out the shape of the subject. In portrait photography, this is a very simple form of lighting that works with most faces that are square to the camera.

Lighting styles in portraiture are generally described with reference to the position of the faces, rather than the camera. Head-on illumination is often called 'butterfly lighting' (because of the shape of the shadow produced under the nose). It remains butterfly lighting if the head is turned at an angle to the camera, providing the light is moved round to retain the shadow under the nose. If the light is moved at an angle to the face, so that a shadow from the nose is thrown across the cheek, you have 'Rembrandt lighting', named after the painter who used a similar shadow effect in many of his masterpieces. A sheet reflector is generally used to add detail to the heavy shadows areas that are formed. With the face in profile, the light can be moved round at right angles to the camera, still giving butterfly lighting. Or it can be positioned round to the side of the face, almost pointing into the camera, to give Rembrandt lighting. Examples of these different types of portrait lighting can be found throughout this book. See if you can find and identify them.

With portraits, the light is usually positioned to emphasize shape. With other subjects, texture can be equally important. As a general rule, the greater the angle between the light and the camera, the stronger the texture. Strong texture lighting can be modified by using a reflector, giving a fine degree of control over the results.

But lighting is essentially a matter of experiment. The modelling light fitted to the flash unit shows you the effect created, provided the studio area is otherwise in darkness (any stray ambient light can make quite a difference to the image you see in the viewfinder and the image recorded on film). Move the light around and study the results. Never be satisfied with a single lighting set-up for any subject — try a range of techniques. And start to study examples of good photography in magazines and advertisements to see if you can make use of the ideas illustrated.

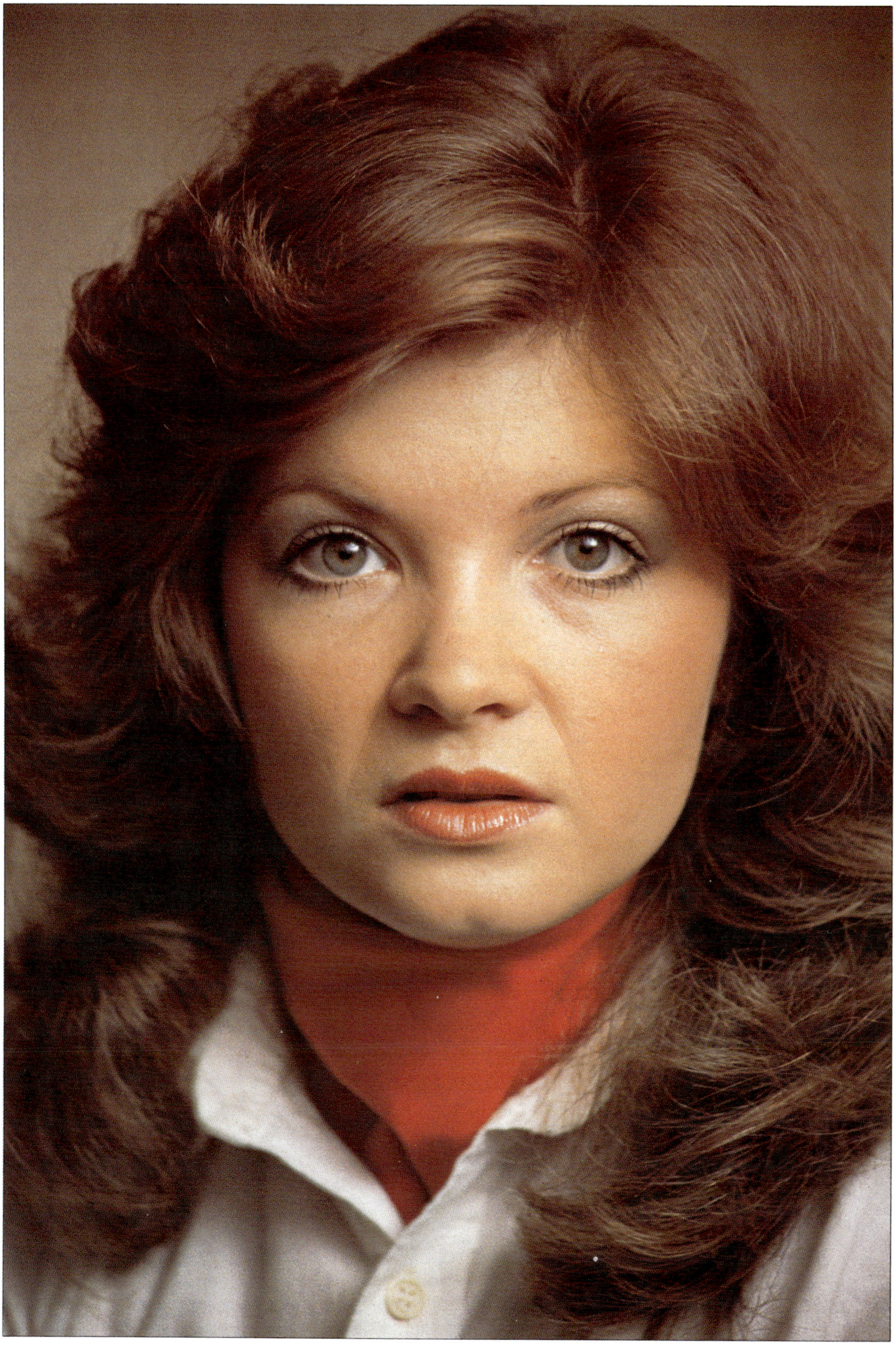

CONTROLLING THE LIGHT

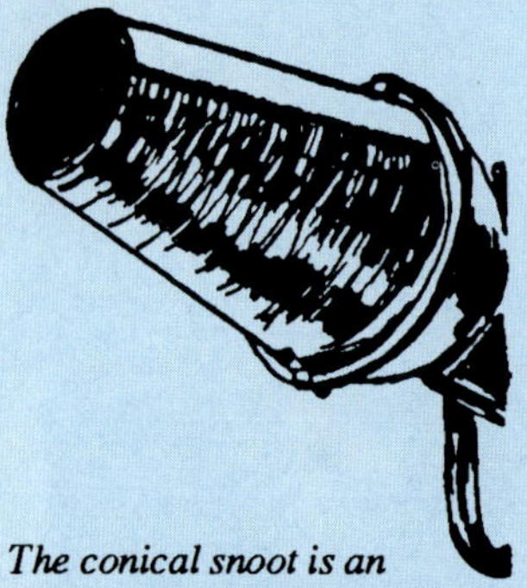

The conical snoot is an effective light baffle, but can be cumbersome for small studio set-ups.

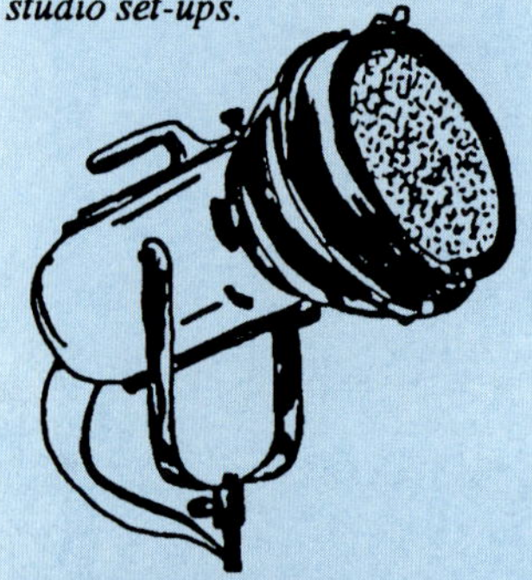

The honeycomb is a more compact version of the snoot, and just as effective.

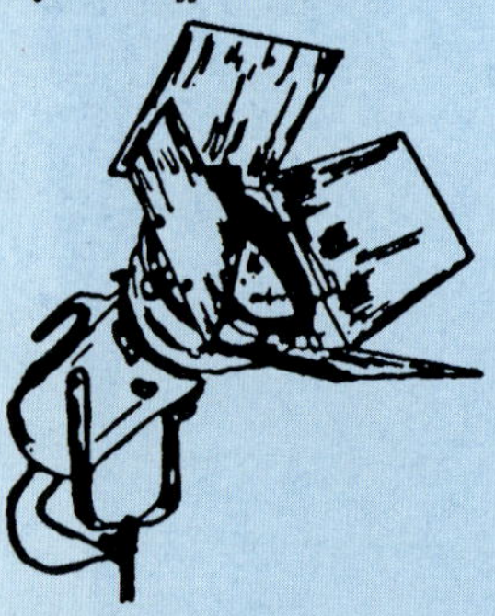

The four-leaf barndoor has two sets of metal flaps which can be adjusted to control the size and shape of the light reaching the subject.

When more than one flash is used, the additional units are often positioned for back or rim lighting. They are aimed towards the subject from the opposite side to the camera, which means there is a good chance of direct light from the flash reaching the camera lens. At best, this will reduce the contrast of the image; at worst it will create streaks of light across the film. Fortunately, there are several ways to eliminate the problem.

Various accessories are available which clip to the metal reflector of the flash unit, restricting the spread of the light. The 'conical snoot' is the simplest. It is a long, shaped tube which produces a narrower beam of light. Although it doesn't really turn the unit into a spotlight, the effect is much the same over distances of just a few feet.

More manageable in small studios are the compact 'honey-combs'. These achieve much the same effect as the snoot in a much smaller accessory by using a honeycomb-mesh of thin metal spacers. When the flash is aimed directly at the subject, there is little loss of light, but the baffles prevent the light from being seen more than a few degrees away from the axis of the beam. This accessory is available with the baffles finished in matt black or shiny silver. The silver gives the more contrasty, more directional light, though there is not a lot to choose between them. A honeycomb is particularly useful for overhead and back lights. It also helps to control the spread of a light used immediately behind the subject.

There are also two types of 'barndoor'. The name comes from the action of two metal flaps, which open and close across the front of the reflector like a pair of doors. The four leaf barndoor has two sets of flaps. These can be adjusted to form a sort of square snoot, or you can close one set down to a letterbox shape for a narrow beam of light. The whole unit rotates for greater versatility. Then there is the single leaf barndoor, which gives a cut-off of light in one direction only. It's designed to attach to a filter holder, but will clip directly to the flash reflector if you are careful. Barndoors are good for rim-lighting set-ups.

Useful though these accessories are, there is an even better way of keeping the light from the lens. Rather than try to control the light at the flash unit, you place a baffle between the flash and the camera. An adjustable reflector is ideal for the purpose. Depending on the angle of the light, it can be placed above the camera lens, or to the side, where it will bounce unwanted light to the ceiling or wall. The advantage of this type of baffle is that it will fully protect the lens from stray light without interfering with the effect on the subject.

Finally, use a good lens hood. Don't rely on a general lens hood — make sure you have the one specially designed for the lens you are using. This will give the maximum protection against flare. Roll-film camera users should consider an adjustable hood. This accessory looks rather like a lens bellows, but fits on the front of the camera. It is racked forward until the edges of the hood are just visible in the camera viewfinder. The hood is then racked back a fraction, giving the perfect length of hood for that particular lens at that particular focus setting.

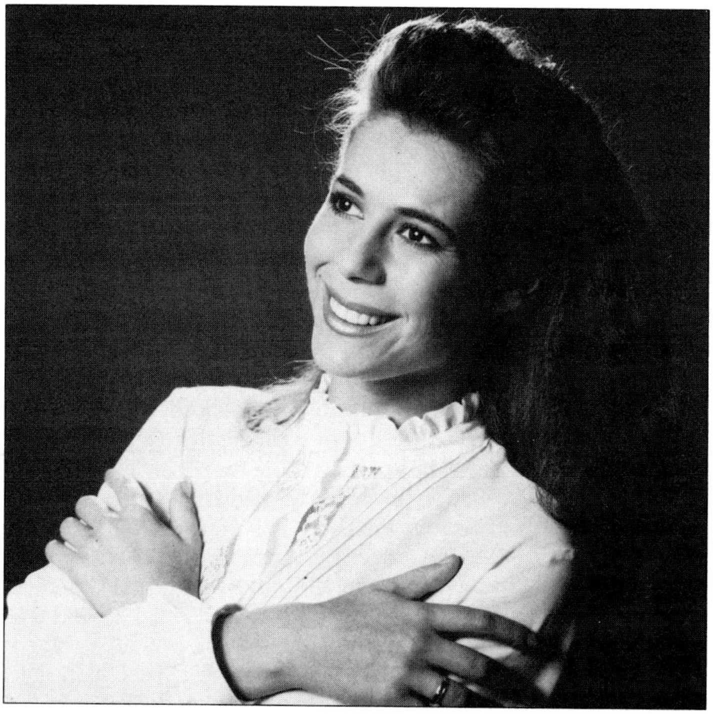

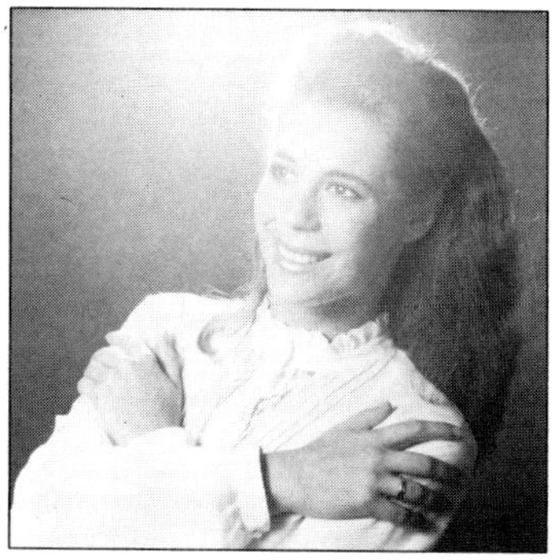

Above: Strong backlighting can create serious flare problems if direct light reaches the camera lens. **Left**: Using an effective light baffle to shield the lens from direct light eliminates the flare patches and increases the overall contrast of the image.

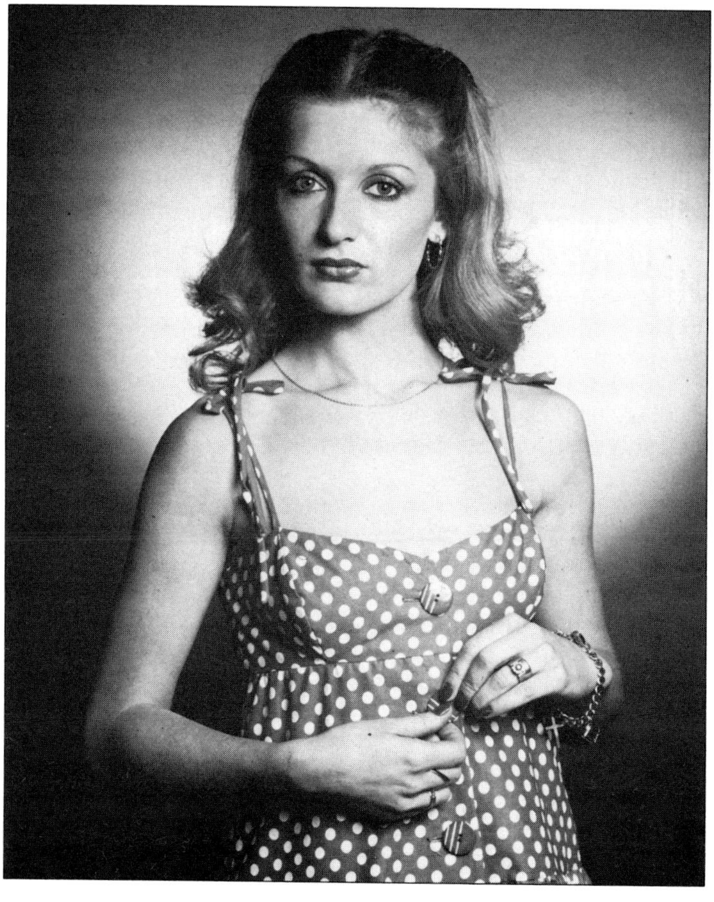

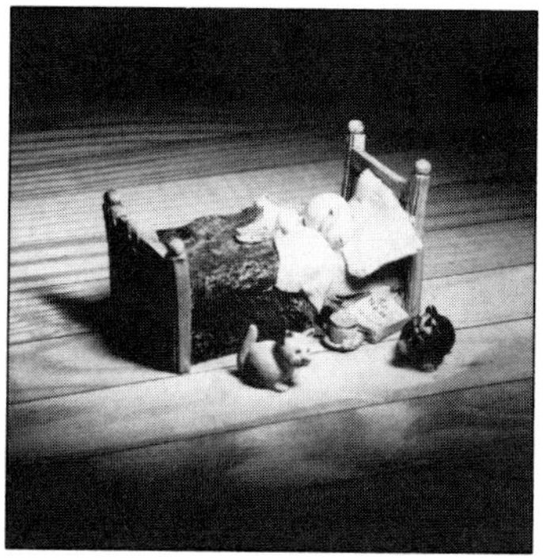

Both the conical snoot and the honeycomb can be used to create a spotlight effect. When used on the background for portraiture *(left)*, the snoot and flash unit can often be hidden from view immediately behind the subject. The closer the unit to the background, the sharper the edge of the light circle. When used as an overhead light for table-top subjects *(above)*, moving the flash unit and honeycomb further away will soften the edges of the circle.

BACKGROUNDS

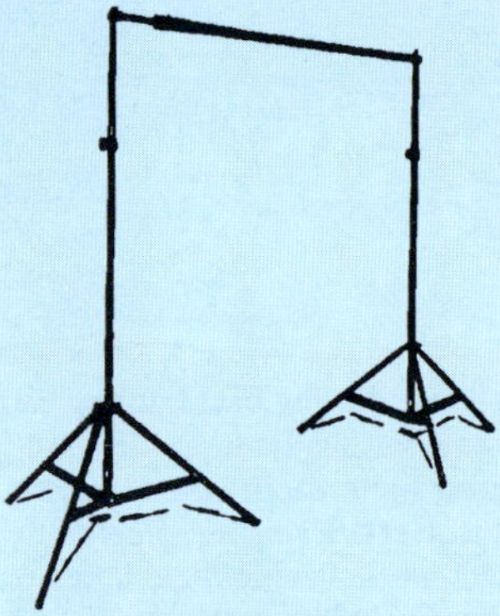

Simple background stands are not difficult to make, but a purpose designed background support will pack away into a small space after use.

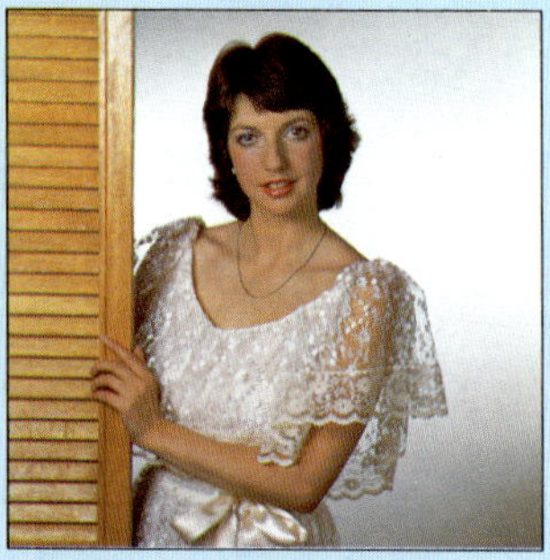

If you start with a white or grey roll of background paper ***(above)****, you can create other colours by placing filter gels over your background lights* ***(below)****. The secret is to make sure that the light on the background is a little less bright than the main lighting, so that you underexpose the colour. This will give you a saturated tone.*

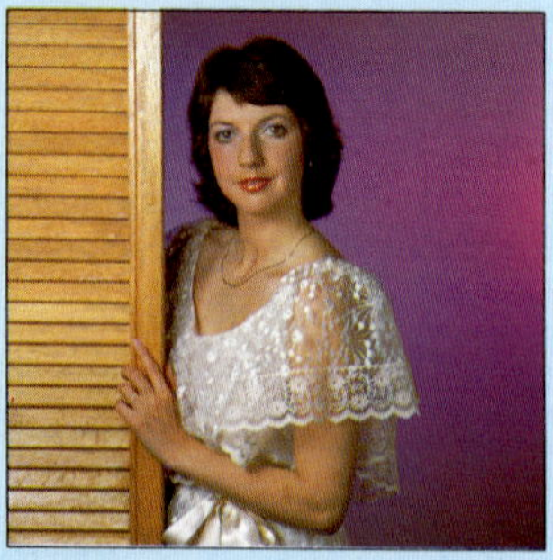

Backgrounds are almost as important as the subject — especially in home studios. They hide the wallpaper, curtains, furniture, ornaments and other everyday clutter that would take the eye away from the centre of the picture.

The most widely used background material is paper. Rolls of a thick paper, specially designed for photographic use and available in a good range of colours, are available from professional photo dealers. The rolls are supplied in two widths. The standard is 3 metres, which is wide enough for full-length portrait work and large still-life studies, but barely manageable in most home studios. More convenient here is the 1.35 metre width, which is ideal for table-top work, and more than adequate for faces and half-length portraits.

Special background stands are available for paper. They support the roll above the camera viewpoint, allowing the loose end to be drawn down. In some shots, the paper is brought down in a curve extending towards the camera, so that the paper is both background and foreground. This is called an 'infinity' background, because there is no obvious break between foreground and background. The paper roll can be quite heavy, so a stable background support is needed for this technique. The same effect can be obtained by fastening the loose end of the paper to a wall and drawing the roll down towards the camera. A few drawing pins or some strips of masking tape will hold the paper to the wall, while the heavy roll lies supported by a table or floor.

Infinity backgrounds can be very effective, especially for still-life shots, but are often difficult to light if there is only a foot or two of foreground. Subject and background tend to receive the same illumination, which is never very satisfactory. The secret of successful infinity backgrounds is space. Extend your foreground as far in front of the background as possible, so that subject lighting can be separated from any background lighting. An alternative to paper backgrounds is the canvas roll. These are available in a range of styles, usually with a handpainted abstract image. Most canvas backgrounds are designed for portrait work, so they tend to have a light central area with a darker edge. Even with very straightforward lighting, they can add a professional touch to pictures. Widths generally start at 6 feet, which can be handled comfortably in a home studio.

But special photographic backgrounds are only the start. For table top work, sheets of 'sugar paper' from stationers are inexpensive but very effective. Buy a range of different colours so that you can pick and choose as you shoot. Do-it-yourself stores will have sheets of thin board finished with timber and brick effects. Curtain and fabric shops will be able to offer a whole range of suitable background materials, from black velvet (ideal for totally black backgrounds) and colourful tracksuit material, to seductive silks and satins.

And then there are the less obvious materials, like shiny black plastic (often sold as groundsheeting) and crumpled aluminium foil. Start looking around with photography in mind and you will soon build up quite a stock of interesting and varied backgrounds.

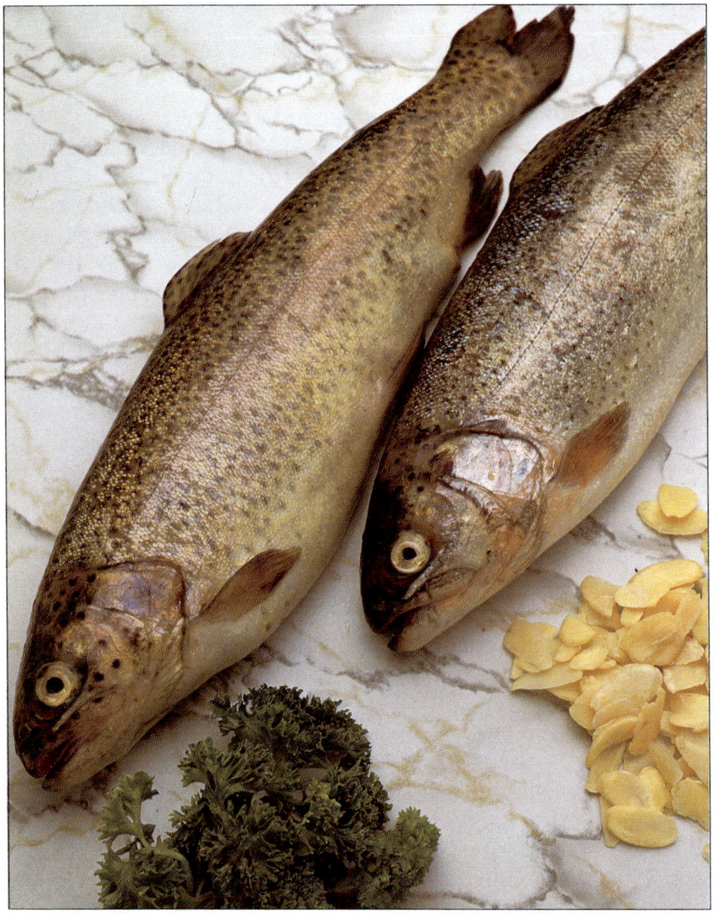

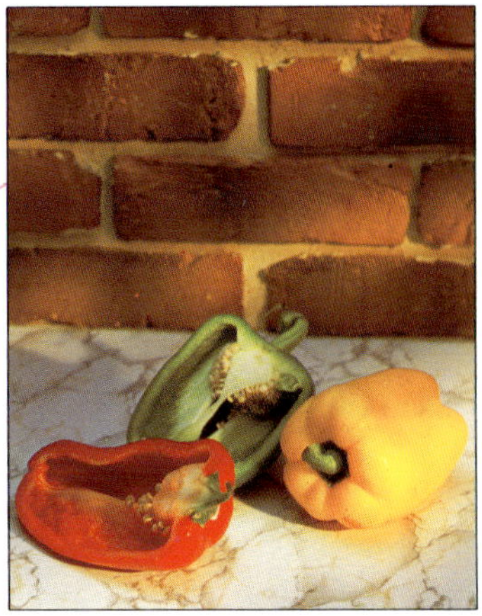

Above: There is plenty of scope for 'faking' backgrounds in photography. The brick wall in this picture is actually a sheet of hardboard panelling with a brick-effect finish. You'll find plenty of similar materials at your local d-i-y superstore.

Left: Many different surfaces can be used as photographic backgrounds. Here, a marble slab is the effective and appropriate surface for fresh trout. A high viewpoint eliminates the real background.

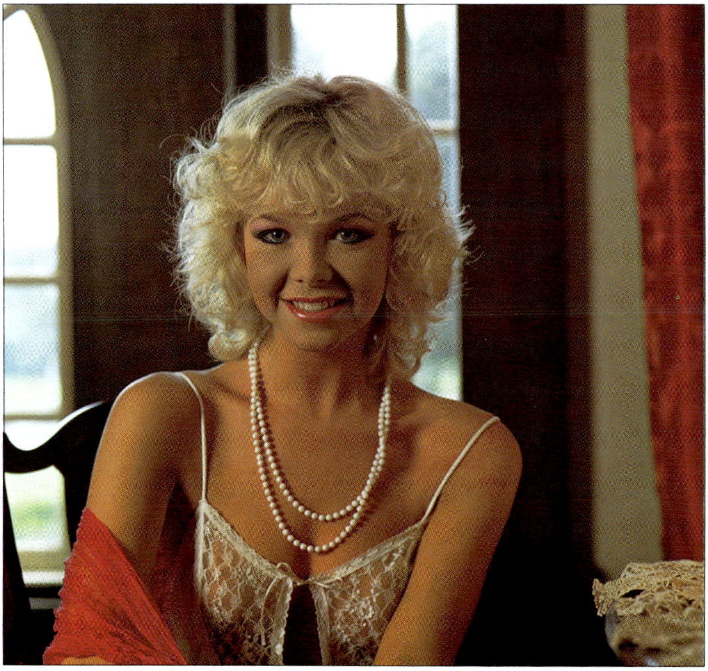

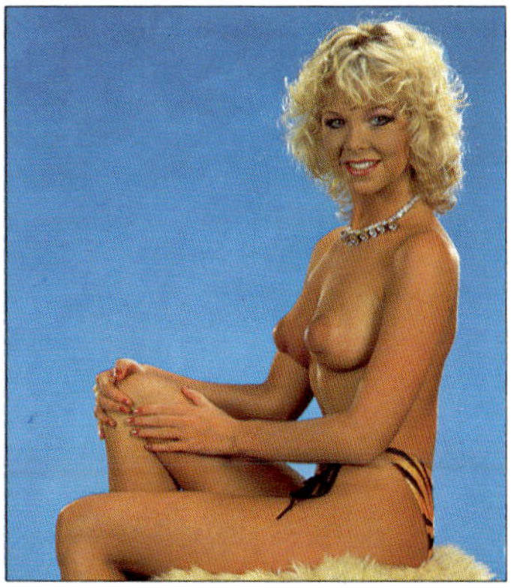

A plain background eliminates any distracting elements and lets you concentrate on the subject (**above**),but using the room surroundings as the background can sometimes add more atmosphere to the image (**left**).

THE BACKGROUND LIGHT

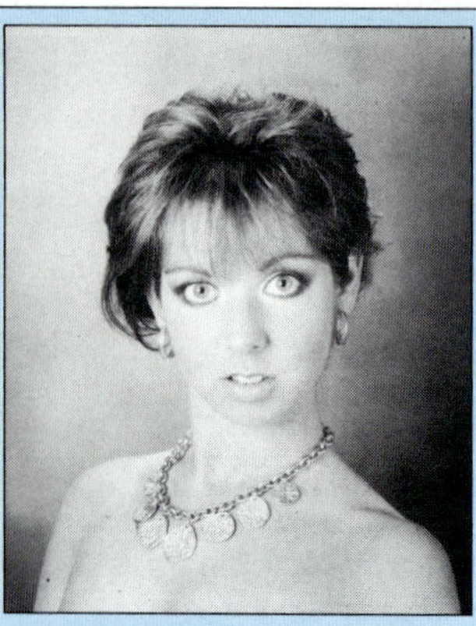

If you shoot portraits against pale backgrounds, you may find the result lacks the impact you want (above). That's because the light surround does not hold your eye in the picture. You can improve the image by having a darker edge to the background (below). If you do your own black-and-white enlarging, it is possible to add the darker surround in the darkroom (as in this example). But if you shoot in colour, especially transparencies, you need to create the darker edge before you expose the film. This can be done by using a snoot or honeycomb on the background light *(see page 36)**, or by shooting against a painted background that features a pale centre and dark edges.*

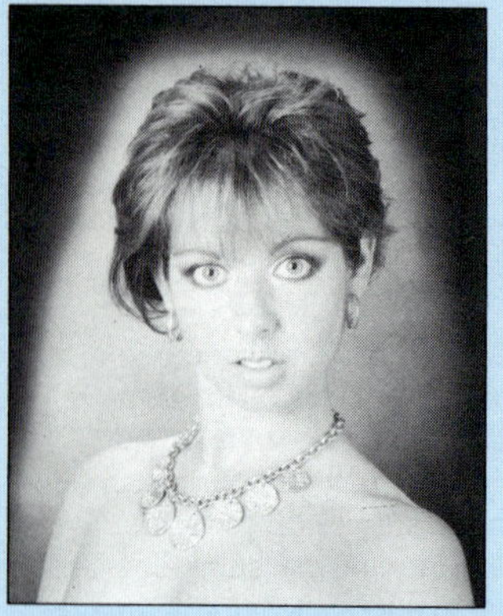

Once the main light has been positioned, you can start thinking about adding a second light. The first question is, do you need one? Every light in a studio set-up should have a specific purpose. Don't decide to use two lights simply because you have two lights. Having made this point, it's true to say that many subjects will benefit from two lights. A single light can leave the image looking rather flat. A second light will add depth. Lighting the background is one way to achieve this effect.

First decide whether you want an even overall light, or a selective illumination. Even lighting is difficult to produce with a single flash, unless your subject is small. The unit needs to be placed at the side of the set, so the far side of the background will receive less light than the nearside. Using the unit with a brolly reflector will help to give more even lighting, but only if you can use the flash several feet away from the background. This can be difficult in a small area. If the subject is small, and on a table, try using the light immediately behind the subject, at less than table height, but angled up. This will give a bright circle of light on the background, and you can position the subject in the centre. If even background lighting is needed for larger subjects, you must use a flash unit on either side of the set.

But is even background lighting essential? In many cases you will produce a more interesting picture by creating areas of light and shade across the background. A single light used off centre gives a background which is brighter on one side than the other. The dark side can be made darker by aiming the flash square at the background, or even turning it away from the centre. If the subject is being lit from the opposite side to the background light, the bright side of the subject will be set against the darker area of the background, while the shadow side of the subject will be against the lighter area of the background.

Portrait pictures often look attractive if the edges of the image are darker than the centre. This helps to prevent the attention from wandering out of the frame. Darker edges can be added when the enlargement is being made, but you will save a lot of time and trouble if you create the effect before exposing the film. Place the flash unit immediately behind the subject, and aim the light at the background. This will give a circle of light. If the circle is too big, move the unit closer to the background, or add the honeycomb *(see page 37)*.

Alternatively, use the flash from the side with the honeycomb fitted. This will produce an oval area of light on the background, but this is just as effective for dark edges to the image. Alter the shape of the oval by using the flashhead very low or as high as the ceiling will allow.

Why use the honeycomb to create the circle of light when the snoot would be a more obvious choice? Because you can fit the filter holder over the honeycomb, but not over the snoot. Your light will probably be quite close to the background and neutral density filters will be needed to prevent gross overexposure. As a general rule, a flash reading taken with the meter pointed forward from the background needs to give the same result as a reading of the main light from the subject position.

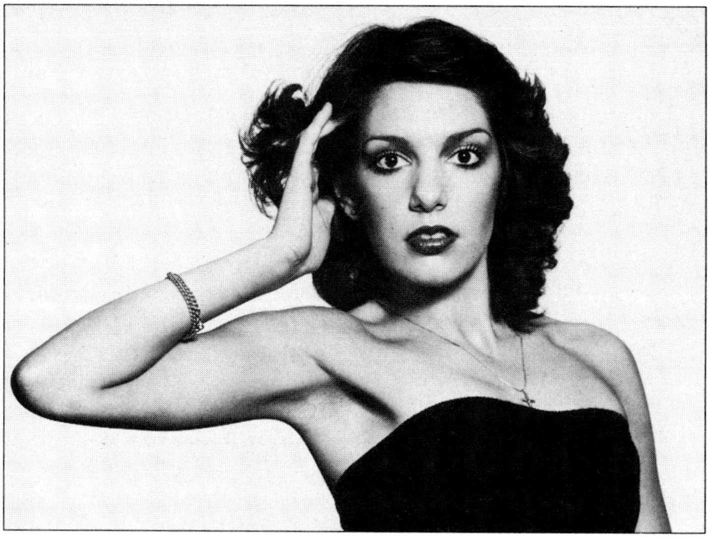

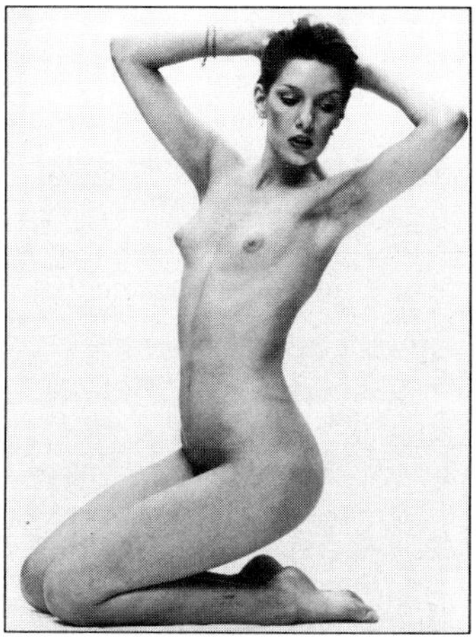

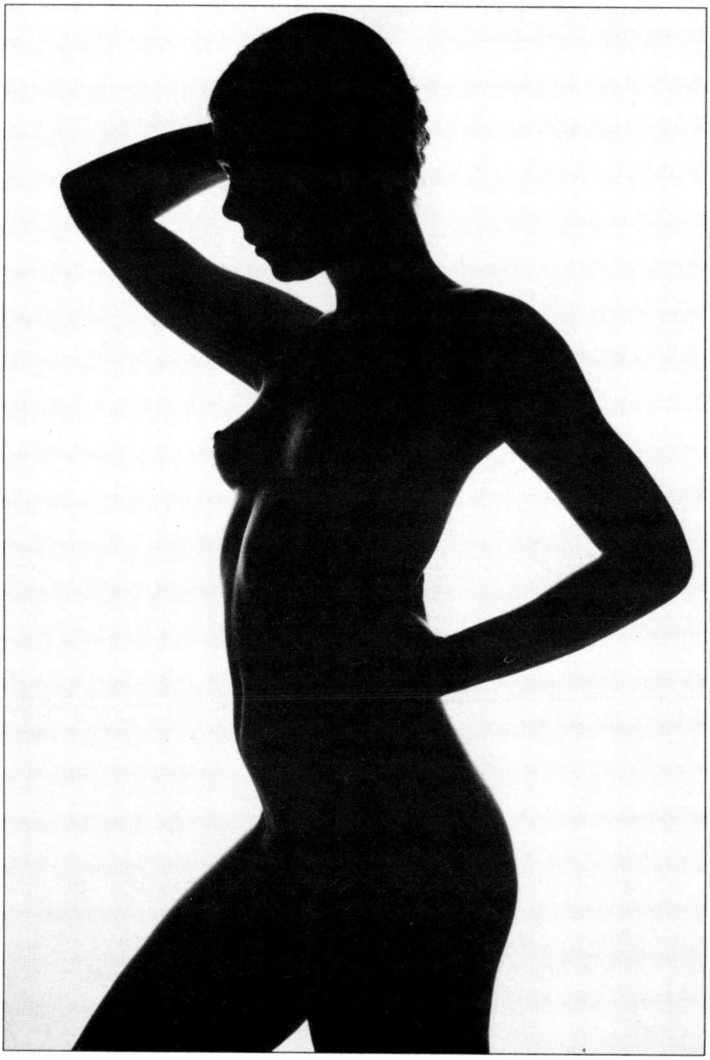

Pure white backgrounds are very difficult to produce when you include all of the subject in your picture. You will nearly always have shadows from the subject across the white surface. The shadows in this picture **(above right)** have been eliminated by using two lights on the subject and two on the background — and by overexposing the background for a high key effect. In a small studio, pure white backgrounds are easier to produce if you work on a more modest scale. Concentrate on half and three-quarter length shots and avoid including the floor. Even so, you will still need two background lights, one on either side, to give an even result **(above left)**. Similar background lighting, but without a light on the subject, is all you need for silhouettes. Overexpose the background by half-a-stop to get a shadowless white. Portrait and figure subjects need to be posed carefully for silhouettes, or you could lose most of the shape (**(below)**. Faces should be in profile, with the hair swept back; angular poses are effective **(left).**

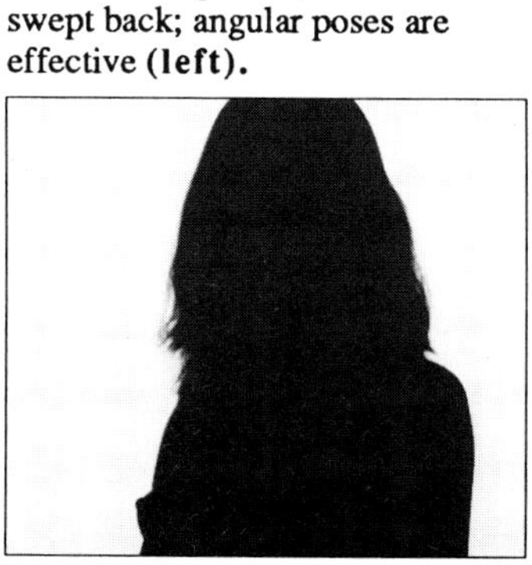

BACKLIGHTING

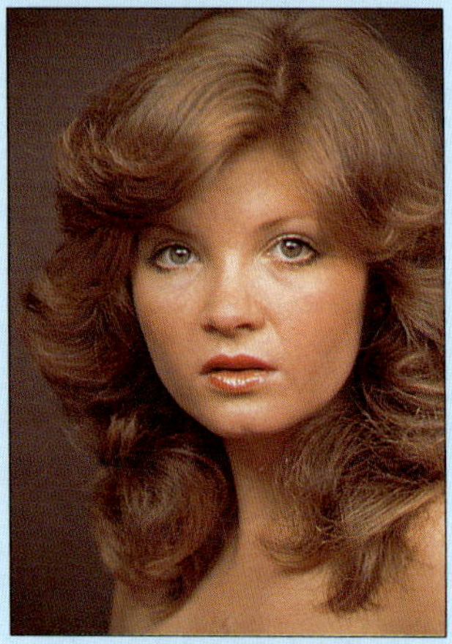

*A portrait without backlighting can look rather flat (**above**). A hair light will separate the head from the background, giving depth to the image. Maximum impact is created by placing the flash unit immediately behind the head, so that a halo of light is formed (**below**). A neutral density filter may be needed on the flash to prevent overexposure.*

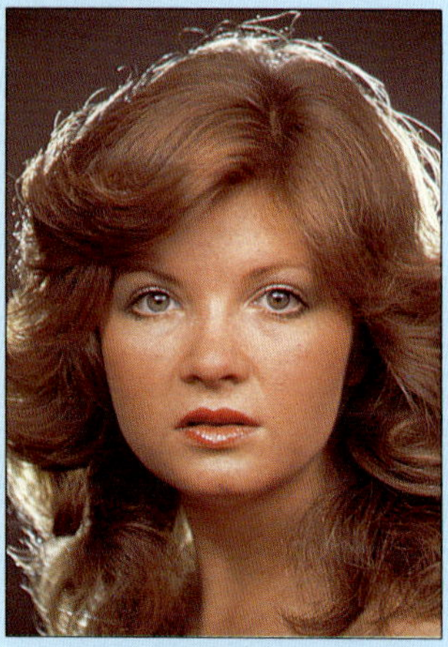

Opposite: Rim lighting can be used on its own, without a front light, for attractive results. Here, two flash units have been used, one on either side of the subject, to create an image in the classical figure style. Light reflected from walls and ceiling gives just a hint of details to the front of the subject.

If you want to add impact to a picture, use backlighting. This is as true for studio photography as it is for daylight shooting. Backlighting separates the subject from the background, giving a three-dimensional quality to the two-dimensional image.

There are a number of effective positions for a backlight. The greatest impact comes from having the light immediately behind the subject and facing forward. Providing the subject is large enough to hide the flash unit, all you will see is a halo of light. This form of lighting is used a lot with pictures of people — particularly glamour portraits. However, it's worth trying with a range of other subjects, too. You may find that the light is so close to the subject that it is impossible to reduce the power sufficiently to prevent overexposure of the halo. This is not a disaster. The effect can still be pleasing.

For a more conventional form of backlighting, place the flash unit to one side of the set, and as far behind the subject as space will permit. Aim the flash at the side of the subject. From the camera position, this will form a rim of light down the side of the subject. By increasing the height of the flash unit, you may be able to extend this rim of light round to the top of the subject. Rim lighting round both sides of the subject can be obtained by using two backlights, one on either side of the set.

An overhead light, coming from the rear of the subject, can be attractive for portraits and many other subjects. Positioning this light so that the support is not seen by the camera can be a problem. In larger studios, a boom arm is used. This is a horizontal bar with the flash unit at one end and a heavy counterbalance at the other, supported on a single extending stand. Versions for small studios tend to be unsteady and are not recommended. Two stands supporting the horizontal bar, with the flash unit hanging from a central clamp provide a much safer overhead light. If you don't have the necessary standard and clamp, the simplest solution is to place the flash unit and stand behind a free-standing background. Extend the stand so that the flash is peering over the top of the background and aim the reflector down at the subject. Fit a honeycomb to prevent an unwanted spread of light.

When you place a second light, whether for lighting the background or for backlighting, switch off the main light. This will enable you to see the effect of the additional light. If the main light is left on, small areas of unwanted highlight from the second flash might not be obvious at the time of shooting — but they will show up on the processed film. The same advice applies if a third light is used. Switch off all other lights until you are happy with its placing. Never have more than one light on while you are making the initial adjustments. Only switch all the lights on when you come to judge the final effect before making an exposure.

Remember to check the balance of the lighting ratios by taking a flash meter reading towards each light in turn. Slight overexposure for rim-lighting is often acceptable, but you could also try underexposing the additional light by about one stop for a more subtle effect.

Direct illumination from the backlight will cause flare in the camera lens. Light baffles are essential *(see page 36)*.

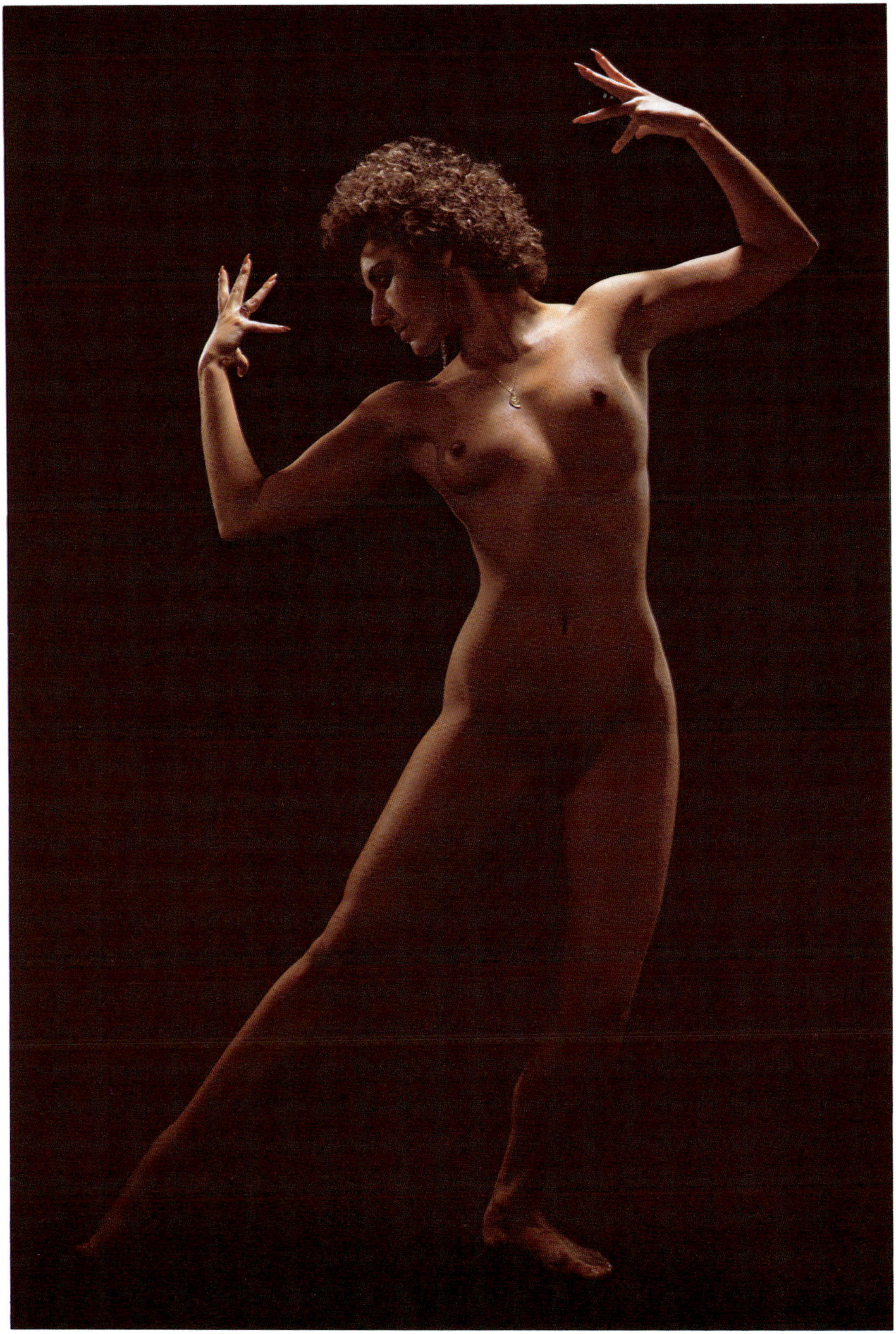

BACKGROUND SHADOWS

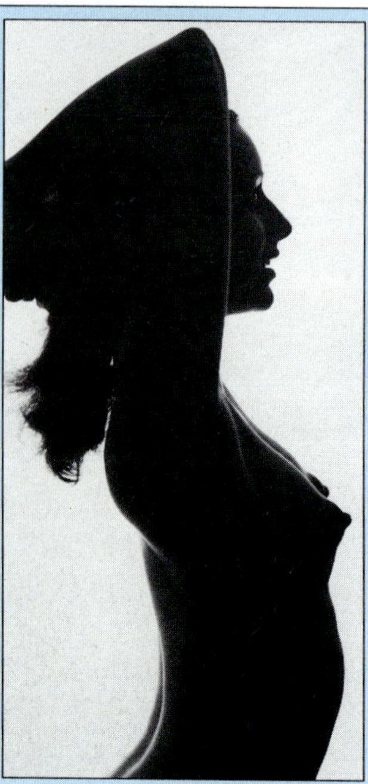

One form of shadowless lighting is the silhouette Generally, you aim light at a white background from both sides and expose for the background. (Take the flash reading by holding the meter immediately in front of the background and then give half-a-stop extra exposure to ensure than any detail is burnt-out). With no light on the subject, you should produce a strong silhouette. But if you are working in a small room, the light from the background will be reflected from the walls and ceiling and will reach the front of the subject. This will make it difficult to obtain a pure black silhouette, so work to the limitations of your set-up and you'll find that you can produce a very attractive grey image (above).

Sooner or later, everyone working in a small studio will come up against the problem of shadows thrown on the background by the subject. Background shadows occur when the subject is close to the background. The easy solution is to increase the distance between the subject and the background. In a small studio, however, this may be impossible.

One technique is to accept the shadow and incorporate it in the picture. A table-top subject with a clear-cut shape may throw a very attractive shadow and the lighting contrast can be increased to make the most of this. You will occasionally come across pictures where the shadow itself is the main subject. A similar technique can also be used with people, placing the subject against the background and using a strong side light to throw a shadow shape down one side.

With larger subjects, it is often possible to fill the camera viewfinder with the subject, so that very little of the background is visible. This is an excellent technique to practice, since many home studio photographers waste their limited resources by including too much background. Even if you do not want to crop right in to the edges of the subject, the close framing will probably eliminate much of the shadow area, giving the impression of a darker area of background, rather than a distinct shadow shape.

If you want to eliminate the shadow completely, the simplest solution is to use a black background. This works well in black-and-white photography, where the background area can be manipulated during enlarging to ensure a rich black tone. Unfortunately, it is difficult to keep light off black backgrounds in small studios and the small amount of reflected light often gives them an unpleasant green cast on colour film.

The obvious solution is to illuminate the background so that the shadow is washed out. This is not as easy as it sounds. There is a good chance of the background light spilling over onto the subject. Use barndoors, a snoot or honeycomb to reduce this risk. The brightness of the background light needs to be controlled carefully so that it matches the main subject light for exposure. Overexposed coloured backgrounds will burn out to white on the film; overexposed white backgrounds will cause flare in the lens and reduce the overall contrast of the image.

One way round these problems is to light the background from behind, rather than from in front. There won't be any spill over of light onto the subject, and the thickness of the background material may well reduce the brightness of the light to avoid overexposure. If the background is not thick enough, sheets of white paper can be attached to the rear to reduce the brightness further. This technique works well with background paper hanging from a free-standing support. For small subjects, very little space is needed behind the background, since the flash reflector can be placed within a few inches of the paper. The result will be a round circle of light behind the subject. This can often be used as part of the composition, giving attractive dark edges to the image. But watch the background — a 100 watt modelling lamp used too close can scorch paper and turn it brown.

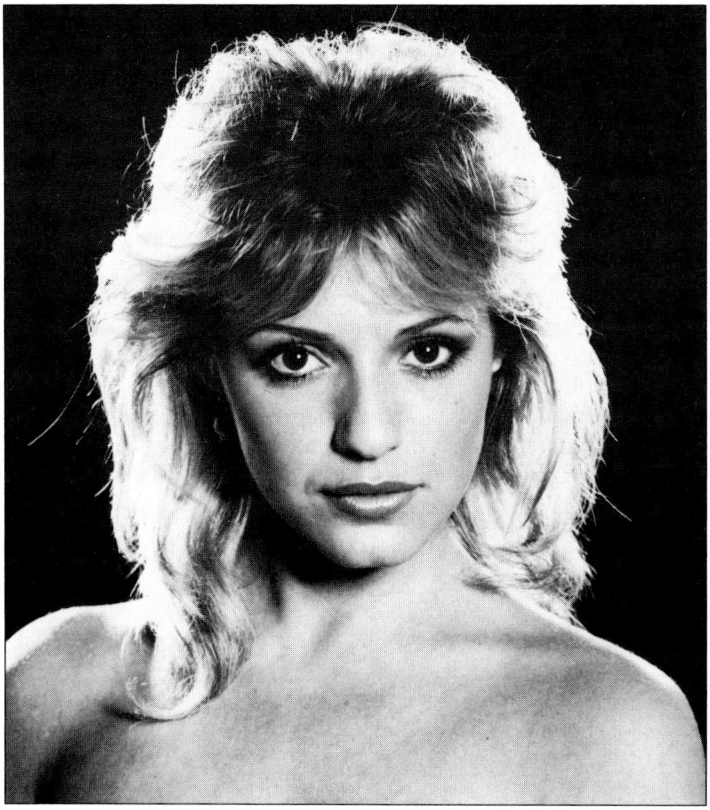

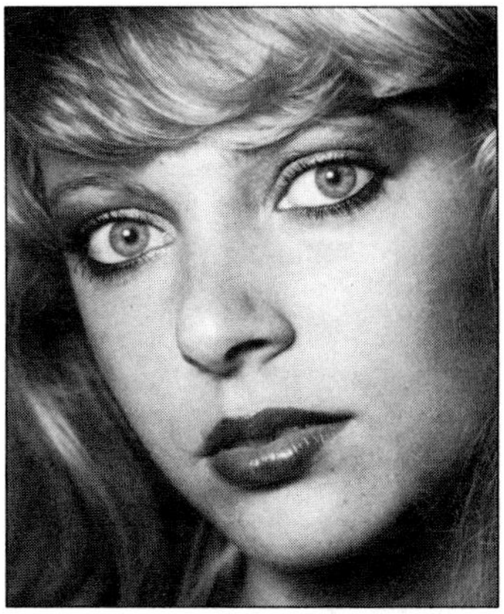

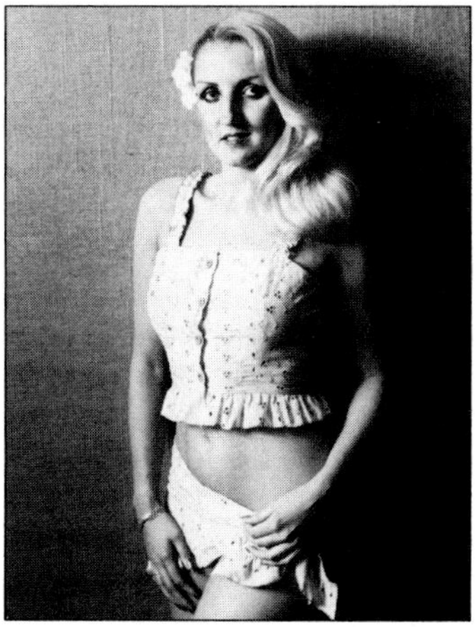

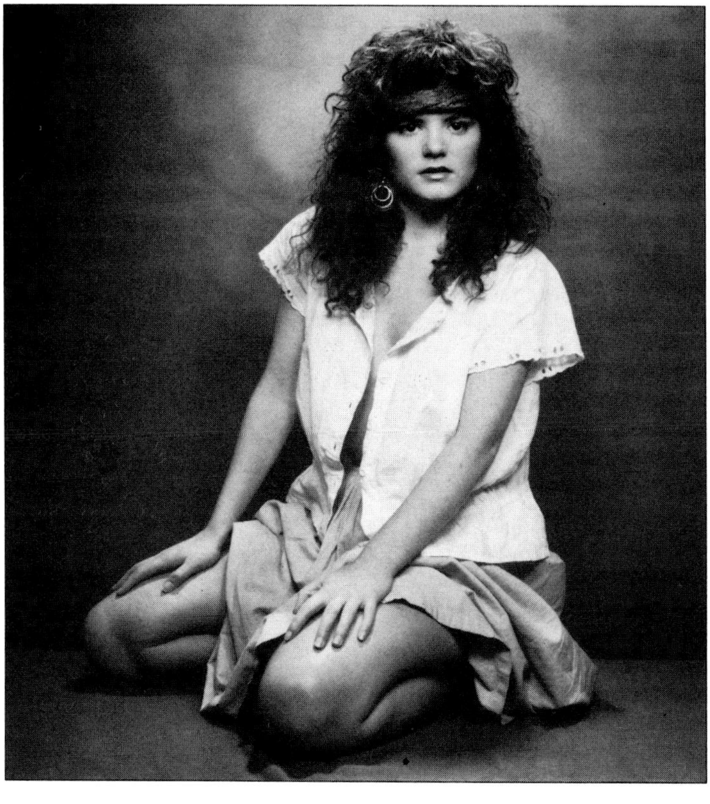

Often, the best way to overcome a problem is to avoid it. If you are working in a small studio area and your main light throws unwanted shadows on the background, move in close so that the subject completely fills the frame **(above top)**. Or use a black background, so that the shadows are not visible **(above left)**. Alternatively, move your subject closer to the background and incorporate the shadow into your composition **(above bottom)**.

If you are shooting glamour pictures and want all of the girl in the picture, avoid the continuous 'infinity' background. It's very difficult to eliminate shadows on this, especially in a small studio. Instead, place a table in front of a vertical background. When the girl poses on this **(left)**, you'll find that the shadows fall off the edge and are less obvious when they reach the background.

FILTERS FOR FLASH AND CAMERA

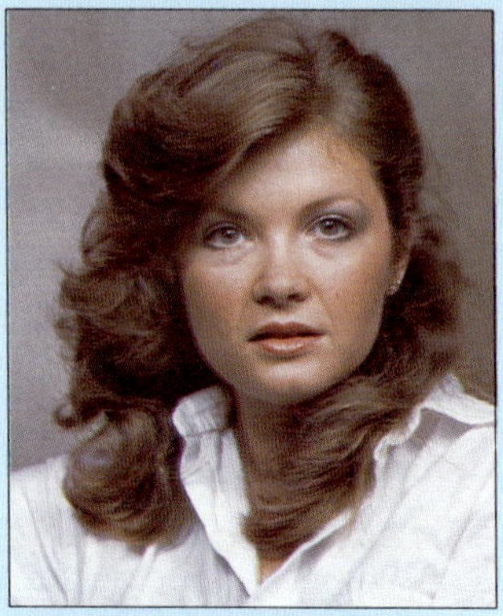

Some films give quite cold results (**above**) with studio flash units. You can produce a warmer image (**below**) by using one of the Wratten 81 series of filters on the lens. Four filters are available — the weakest is the 81A, followed by 81B, 81C and 81EF. The 81EF was originally designed to correct the excessive blue of some electronic flash units. However, most units now have built-in correction, so the 81EF should only be used when you want a very strong warming effect. Generally, an 81A or 81B is adequate. Many filter manufacturers quote the Wratten number where they have an equivalent filter in their range. If not, choose a pale warming filter.

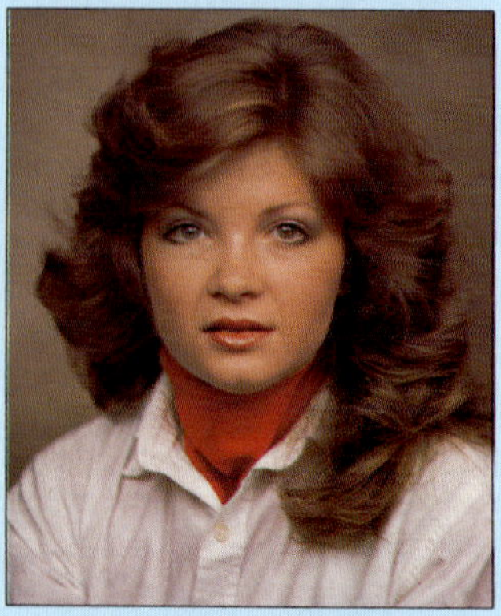

There are two basic types of filters that can be used for studio photography — those that make a picture look normal, and those that make it look different. Examples of both types can be used on the flash unit or on the camera.

Special filter holders are available for most flash units. They are usually designed with plenty of space between the reflector and the filter. This allows air to circulate freely and avoids overheating. The filters are flexible sheets of flame-proof material which either clip to the holder, or stay in place with small magnets. Filter 'gels' (from the days when they were made of 'gelatine') come in a range of colours, but the most useful are the neutral density filters. These reduce the brightness of the light without affecting its colour and are invaluable for balancing the background or backlight with the main light. You should have a filter holder and at least a couple of neutral density filters for every flash unit apart from the first, unless there are at least three different power settings available on the flash control panel.

Coloured gels give attractive pastel shades when the flash is used as a background light. White background paper is not essential for this technique — interesting effects are produced by using coloured gels with grey and pastel background papers. Make sure that the background light matches the main light for brightness. Overexposure of the background flash will wash out the colour. You may need to use the neutral density gels with the coloured gels.

Coloured gels can also be used with backlighting. A coloured rim of light around the subject can be very attractive. However, this is a technique which only retains its effectiveness when used occasionally.

Even without flash gels, you might find that some of your colour photographs have a slight colour cast. This is because the film may not be balanced precisely to the colour temperature of the studio flash. There is no need to change films — you can use a filter on the camera instead. The 81 series of filter are very useful. The 81A is the weakest, followed by the 81B and 81C. They are pale orange in colour. This eliminates the slight blue cast which often occurs when using studio flash. The strongest of these filters often overcorrects the cast, but the warm-toned image it produces is very flattering for portraiture and glamour pictures. For an even stronger 'suntanned' image, try the 81EF filter. Most filter manufacturers include these filters in their ranges, though not always with the same designations.

A good soft-focus filter is useful for some portraiture. In addition to hiding minor skin blemishes and subduing wrinkles, it can create a romantic mood. Don't confuse diffuser and pastel filters with soft-focus. The best type of soft-focus filter has a series of tiny lenses ground into glass filter. The effect it produces cannot be reproduced by any other type of filter.

Camera effect filters should be used very sparingly with studio photography. You have full control over the subject in front of the lens, so there should be no need to seek extra impact by adding a filter to the lens. And remember that effect filters are only effective when used infrequently.

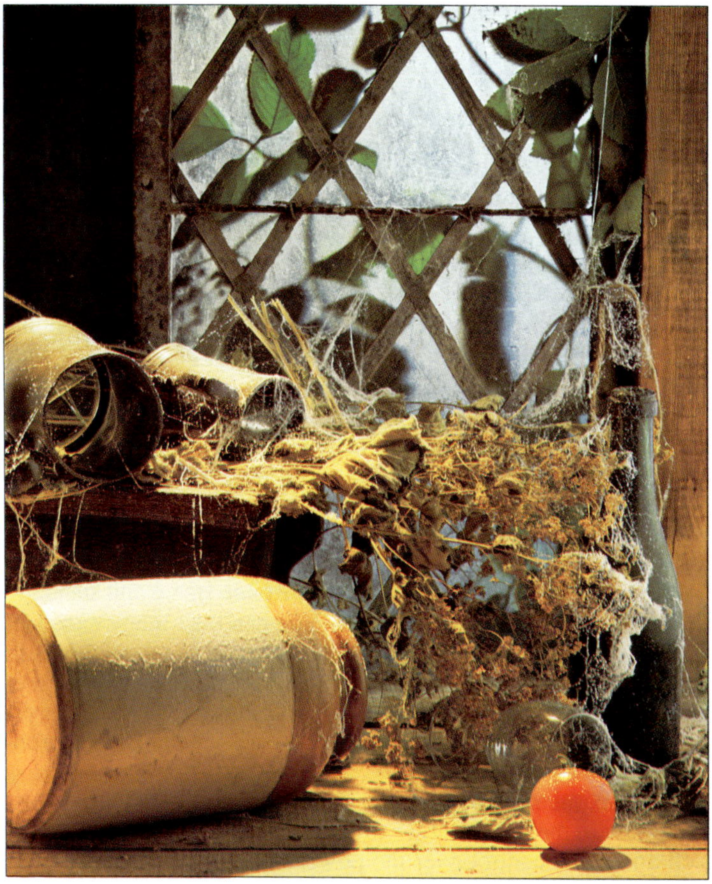

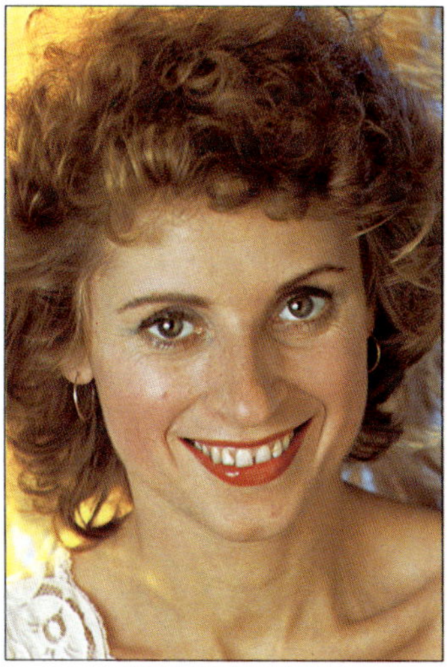

Above: Filter gels can be used on hair lights to add a little colour to the backlighting. Soft pastel shades are usually more satisfactory than strong colours. Here, two hair lights were used, one with a yellow filter, the other with a steel blue filter. While adding colour, the filter gels absorb some of the light, reducing the risk of overexposure from the hair lights.

Above left: This is a studio set, lit entirely by flash. The 'daylight' coming through the window is created by a flash unit fitted with a steel-blue filter gel. The warm interior light is from a similar flash unit fitted with a yellow-gold filter gel. Controlling the colour of the light in this way can add a lot of atmosphere to an image. With careful use of filters and diffusers, you can create images which appear to have been lit entirely by daylight. Incidentally, this still-life was set up in just a few hours. The 'cobwebs' have been sprayed on from a can!

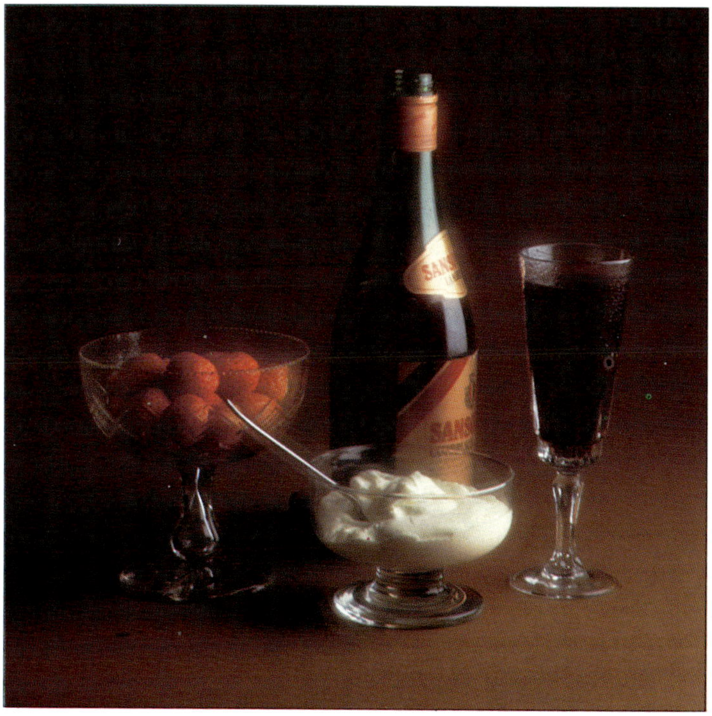

Below left: Sometimes, photographs can be too sharp. This low-key still-life set-up has been photographed with a soft-focus filter to take the hard edge of the bottle and glasses. The filter also softens the light. A wide range of soft-focus filters are available. Try different types until you find one that gives the effect you require.

STUDIO OUTFITS

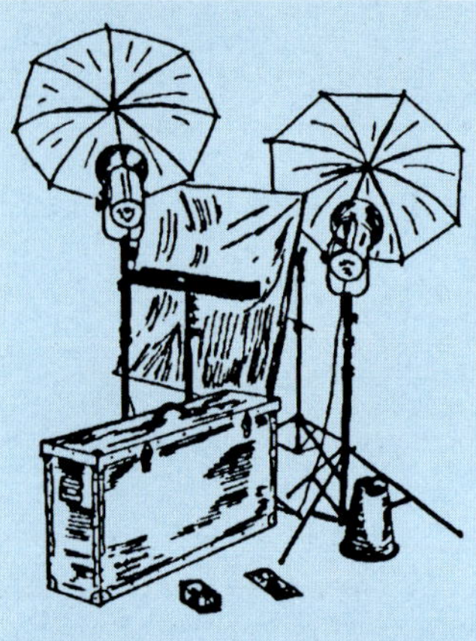

You can start your studio flash system with just a single light and stand, or buy a studio outfit containing several flash units, plus other accessories. The outfit can be cheaper than buying all the items separately. However, even if you buy a complete outfit, don't feel that you have to get value for money by using every flash unit for every picture you take. There are times when a picture needs three or or four flash heads — but there are also many times when you will produce the best results with just one or two units.

Opposite: This picture used the most lights and accessories you are ever likely to need in a small studio set-up. The main light is from the front, with a brolly reflector. Behind, on either side, is a flash head used direct, but fitted with a filter holder and a neutral density filter to reduce the power. These two units are producing the rim-lighting round the body.A fourth flash head is aimed down from above the background to produce the rim lighting around the top of the head. Finally, there are three reflectors shielding the camera lens from direct flash illumination.

There is no ideal lighting outfit for the home studio. Every photographer will have different ideas as to what is essential. Initially, all you need is a single basic studio flash unit. You don't need tremendous power in a home studio, so a unit towards the lower end of the range will be adequate. Neither do you need extras like a built-in slave cell, or variable power settings, since the main unit is always connected by cable to the camera, and always used at full power.

Buy at least two camera synchronization cables — they can fail at any time and might leave you in the middle of a photo session with no means of firing the flash.

Buy a lighting stand that will enable you to raise the flash unit right up to the ceiling. A three-section stand is usually suitable.

If you are going to concentrate on table-top photography, a window light diffuser might be the most useful accessory for your basic outfit. This can be used with polystyrene reflectors. For portraiture, a silver brolly reflector is probably more suitable, together with a sheet reflector with adjustable frame and stand.

That completes the basic outfit. You can take many excellent pictures with a single light and a reflector, and it's a good idea to restrict yourself to this set-up until you are proficient in its use. Additional lights and accessories will not improve your photography, though they will enable you to tackle a wider range of techniques.

The next item to buy is a second flash unit and stand. These can be similar to the first. Useful extras are a built-in or accessory slave cell and some control over the power of the flash output. If you decide to buy a more powerful flash unit, this should become your main light, with the weaker unit used as the secondary flash. The slave cell means that you should not need any extra connecting leads.

With two lights, it is time to think about a flash meter. This is by no means essential, but it will help you to obtain consistent results, and is particularly useful for balancing the second light with the main light.

At this stage, you should also be thinking of a light baffle, such as a honeycomb or a set of barndoors, plus a filter holder and set of filter gels. Another sheet reflector and stand would also be very useful.

From this point on, you will probably start to buy additional lighting accessories as you feel the need for them during studio sessions. A floor base or a low level mounting bracket for one of the flash units is very handy for illuminating the background from a low angle. A background support system will hold paper rolls and overhead lights.

Many photographers will find that two flash units are enough for home studio photography. Finding enough space to set up a third stand can be a problem in small areas. However, the ideal home studio outfit probably has three flash units. You may not need the third light very often, but it is useful to have it available for the times it is required. Four flash units are only going to be useful in the larger home studio area and the fourth unit is only worth adding to the outfit when you have all the other accessories you need.

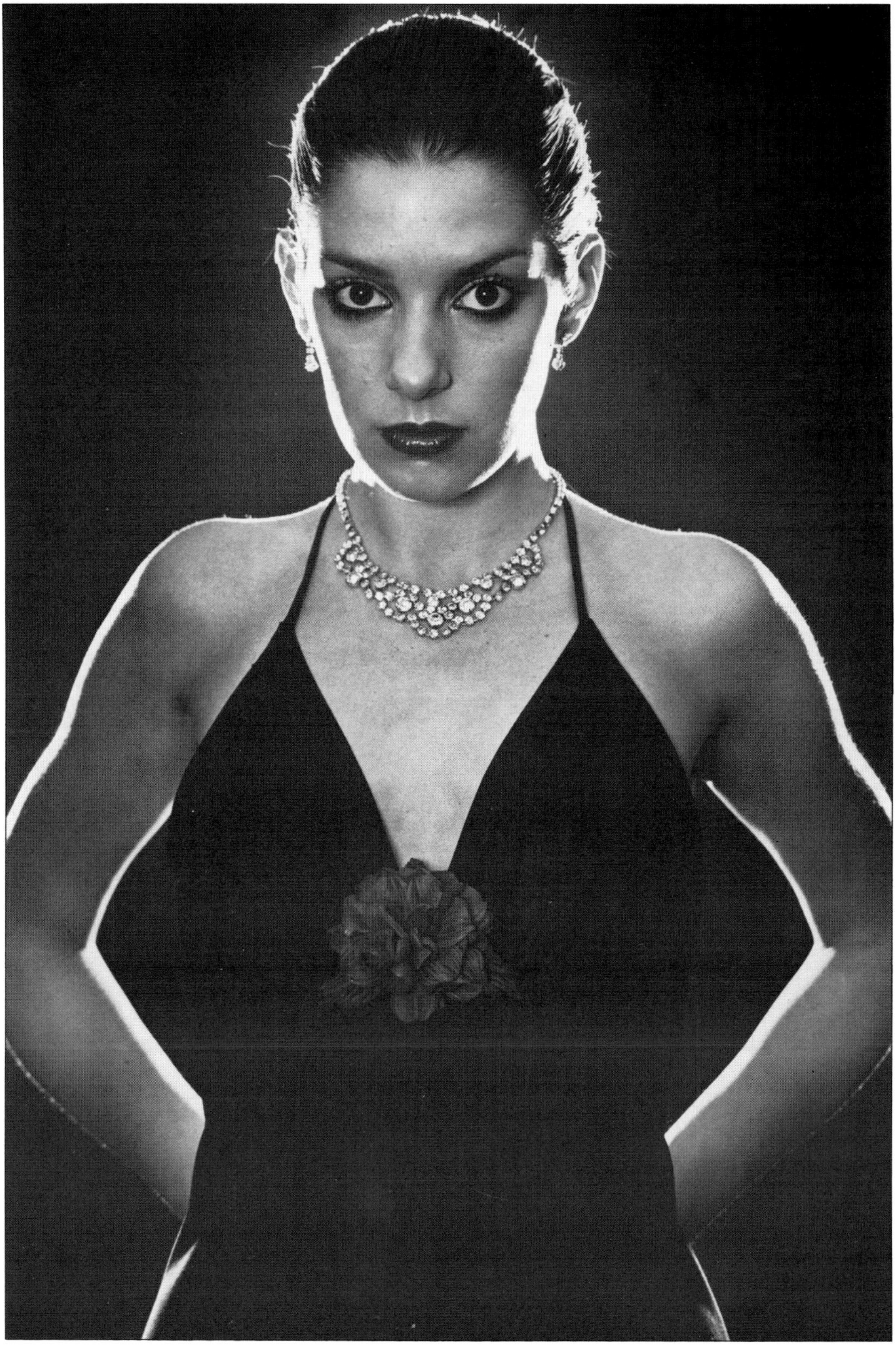

THE STUDIO BOOTH

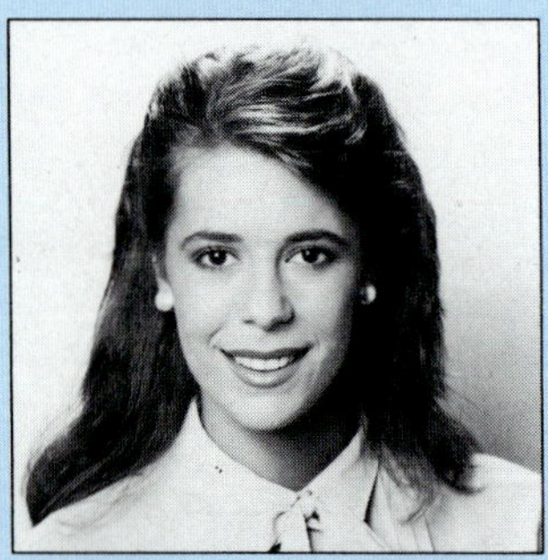

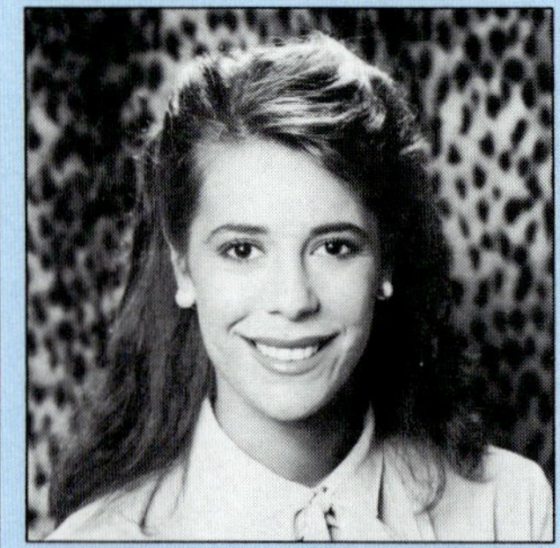

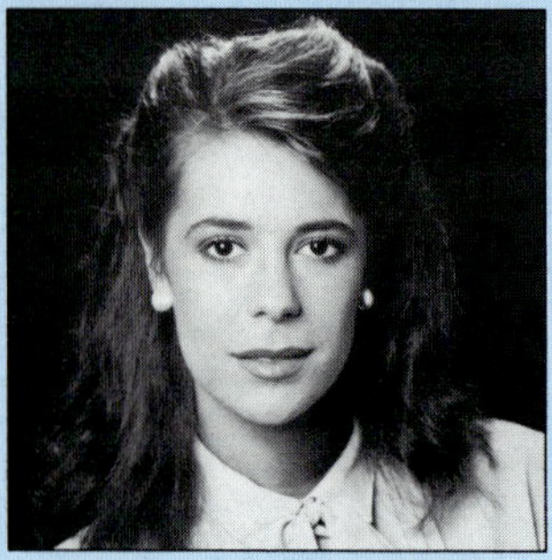

The studio booth is a simple idea that can be adapted to suit any space. It can be set up in a living room or bedroom, garage or workshop. You might even be able to fit it into a narrow hallway, using white walls as the sides. And it is quite easy to put together a studio booth from portable accessories so that you can take it around to other houses for portrait work. Although the basic lighting remains much the same, you can add variety to the pictures by changing the background (above).

After a few studio sessions, you will start to build up a repertoire of lighting set-ups which give good results. Here is one to add to your collection. It gives a soft, shadowless illumination which is ideal for female portraiture. It also works well for any subject where you need to show detail.

The 'studio booth' set-up is basically a cubicle of white surfaces, with one wall missing. However, there is no need to build anything elaborate. A projector screen makes an ideal back wall, though a sheet of material or a large sheet of card would do just as well. The two side walls can be sheet reflectors. If you are shooting portraits, reflectors a couple of feet square are more than adequate.

The secret of the studio booth is the 'floor'. The ideal accessory for this is a small white drawing board. For a portrait, place this in front of the subject, at about waist-level, with the board at an angle of about 30°. Your subject is now fully enclosed by white reflector surfaces. (If you can't lay your hands on a drawing board, don't worry, any flat white surface that can be set at an angle to the subject will be just as good, though probably not quite as convenient. If necessary, you can even get your portrait sitter to hold a white board in front of themselves, at the correct angle!)

You can work with a single light. The position is not critical, but to one side of the camera, and a couple of feet higher than the lens, works well. For portraits, get the subject to turn their head towards the light, so that you have fairly flat lighting on the face. Don't worry about the lighting being too flat for portraits. This set-up is best for beauty shots, where the basic shape of the face is created by the make-up – the lighting merely complements the effect.

For the best effects from the studio booth, you need a second flash unit. This should be positioned behind the back wall of the booth, with the flash head supported above the wall and angled down to shine on the back of the subject. In portraiture, this is called a hair-light – for other subjects it's a backlight. The main purpose of this light is to put a rim of illumination around the subject and separate it from the background. In the studio booth, however, it also acts as a fill-in light, since light is reflected off the angled surface of the drawing board and lightens any shadows at the front of the subject.

As with any basic idea, there are plenty of ways to alter the set-up to suit different subjects – you don't want all your pictures looking the same. Instead of a white background, you can use black, or a colour. Be careful with bright colours, however, since light bouncing off the background onto the side wall and then onto the subject can caused slight colour casts. Shiny reflective backgrounds can be effective here, especially if you shoot at wide apertures, so that highlights in the background appear out-of-focus in your photographs.

Try covering the drawing board with aluminium foil, shiny side up, or even place a large mirror on the surface. This will reflect the backlight into the face for portrait shots, giving a 'glow' to the features. (If you always thought that girls shown in beauty shots were just incredibly healthy, sorry to disappoint you. A lot of the effect comes from make-up and lighting.)

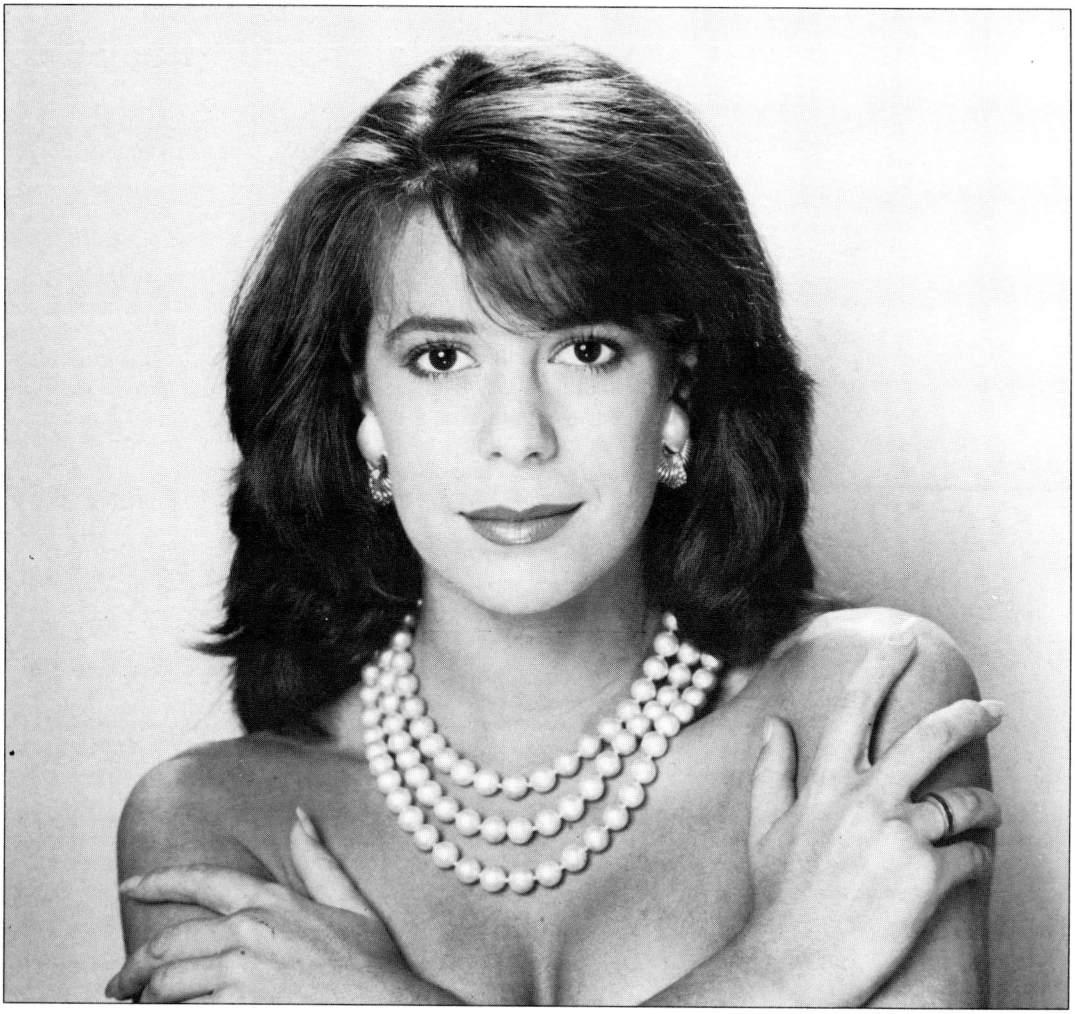

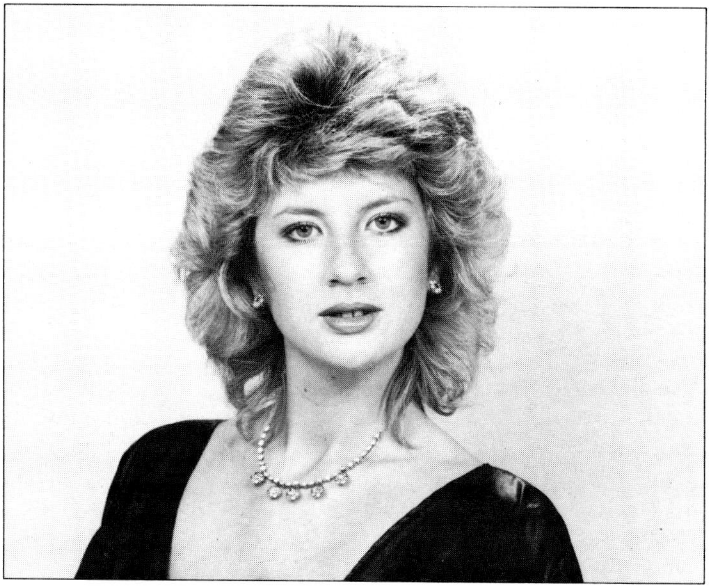

Above: The studio booth is ideal for female portraiture. It produces a very soft, glamorous lighting, with plenty of soft illumination to fill-in the shadows under the eyes and chin. In this photograph, a mirror has been placed on a drawing board in front of the girl, reflecting illumination from the backlight into the face. This gives an extra 'glow' to the skin.

Left: If you have a second flash unit, always use it as a backlight in this set-up – it helps to separate the subject from the background and gives depth to the image. Although studio booth lighting is going to be much the same for all your pictures, at least you can be sure of attractive, consistent results.

THE TABLE-TOP STUDIO

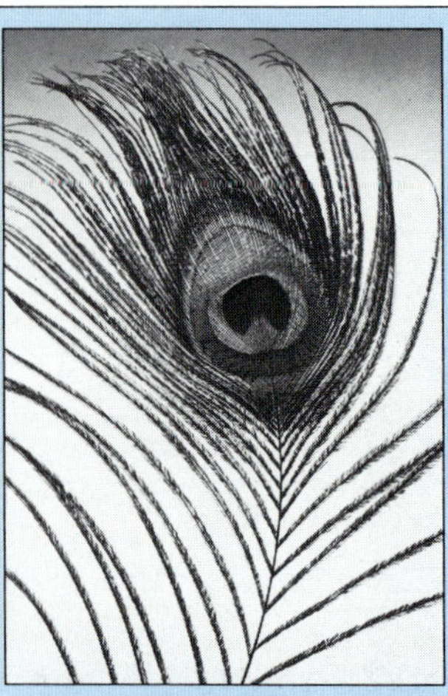

A table-top studio can be fitted into the smallest corner of our house. Here, a peacock feather is supported in front of a white background and lit with a single flash. Top quality results like this are easy when you work within the limitations of your space and your equipment.

Table-top photography is possible in almost any room in any house. All you need is a small area for the subject, plus a few square feet for the camera and flash units. 'Table-top photography' is a general term used when working with small subjects, but the description is usually fairly accurate for the home studio – a small table offers the most convenient surface for the subject. Most photographers use this sort of set-up for still-life photography, but it is just as suitable for the indoor photography of insects and small animals.

In many ways, the table-top studio is just a miniature version of a larger studio. A lot of small subjects are photographed against an infinity background. This is simply a roll of paper, or a large sheet of card, curved round in a continuous length to form both the background and the base. Since the table-top studio is a lot smaller than a full-size studio, the infinity background is much easier to handle.

A variation is the studio workbench. This is generally a light-weight metal frame fitted with a sheet of curved white perspex. The perspex can be lit from underneath to give a bright, shadowfree background to the subject. It's also possible to use filter gels with the rear lighting to introduce background colour effects. If you intend to do a lot of table-top photography, one of these benches, although quite expensive, is well worth considering – though you might be able to improvise with a glass-topped coffee table. Another expensive item worth looking at is the graduated background. This is a large sheet of wipe-clean material which starts with strong colour or neutral tone at one end and fades to white at the other. Used carefully, it can create an excellent impression of depth in your pictures, and adds interest to what might otherwise be a plain background.

Even with small scale photography, it helps to have a distance of two or three feet between the subject and the vertical part of the infinity background. This allows the background to be lit separately from the subject. The alternative is to cover the table top with material and hang a separate background some distance behind. This allows you to illuminate the background from below table height, creating an area of highlight which holds attention to the centre of the frame.

Lighting for table-top subjects can be extremely simple. Often, a single flash unit and a reflector is all you need. A diffused light directly above the table can give very attractive lighting to many subjects, particularly if the table is covered with a light-toned material to reflect light back into the underside shadows. If a second light is available, then it can be used on the background, or as a backlight.

Table-top photography can range from a simple product shot of a small box or bottle, to complex minature sets that take weeks or months to assemble. Techniques that can be used include close-up photography, perspective control and multiple masked exposures – not to mention a multitude of simple but dramatic lighting effects. It's an area of photography that can be all-absorbing, especially if you have a talent for model-making, or for creating attractive compositions from a collection of small items.

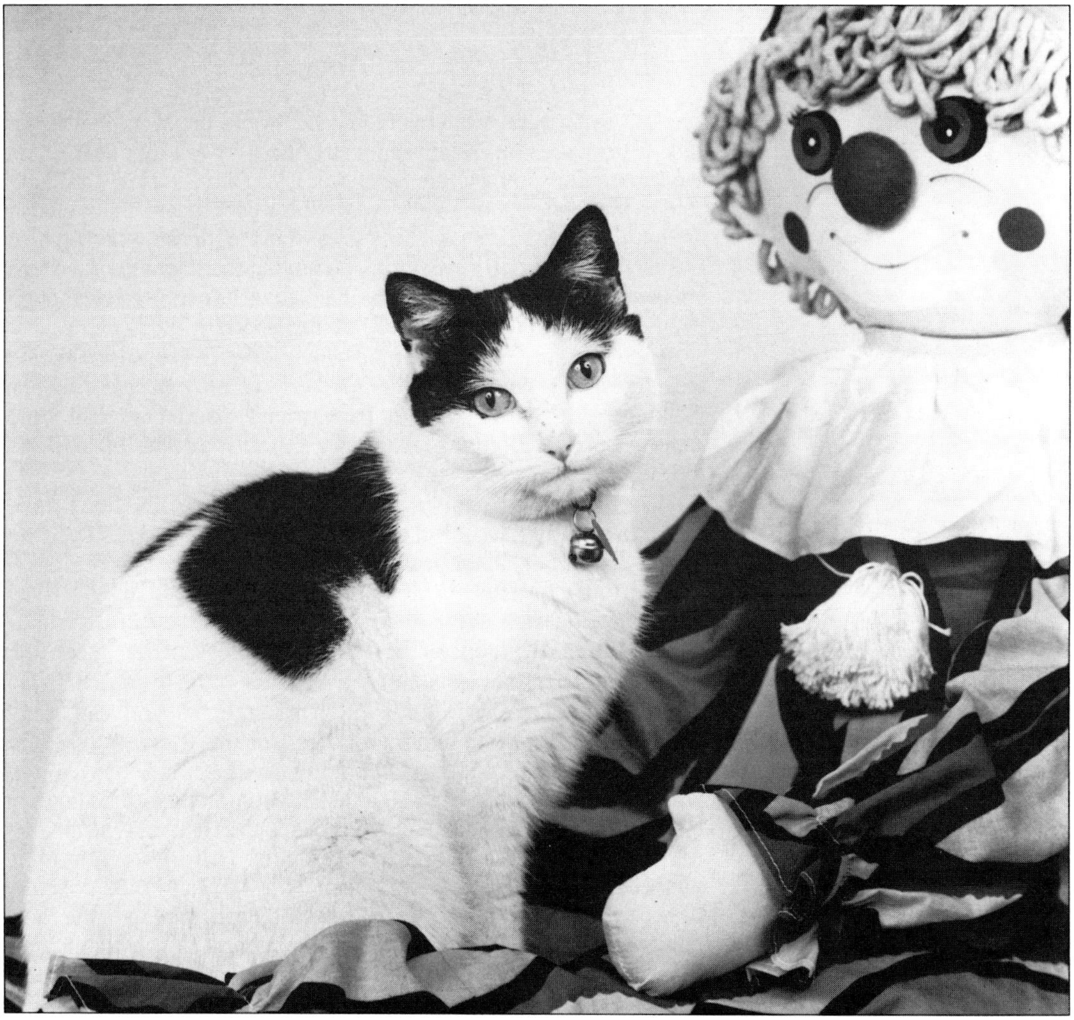

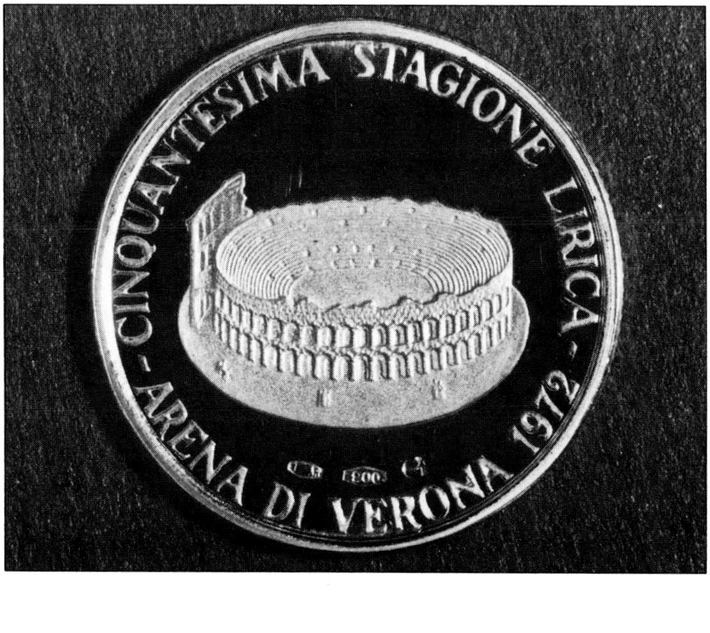

The table-top studio can be used for a wide variety of subjects. The cat and clown *(above)* were shot in the set-up used for the studio booth pictures *(see previous page)*, except that here the drawing board reflector becomes the table-top. The tiny coin *(left)* has a small sheet of card as the background. A single flash is used from the right side to emphasise the texture and detail.

THE DOORWAY STUDIO

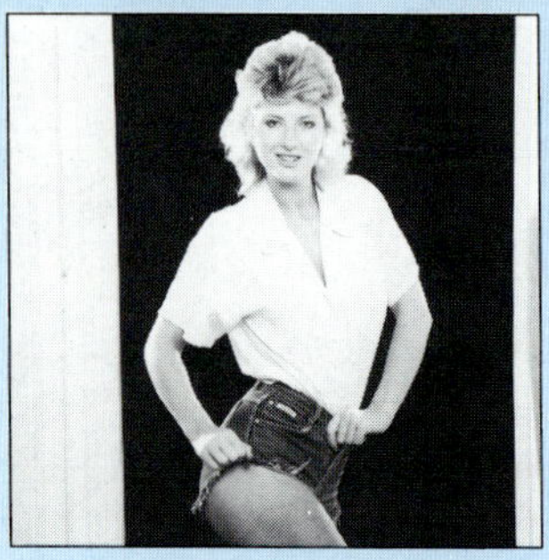

This is the picture which shows how all the photographs opposite were taken. You can see the door frame on either side of the girl. It connects a narrow hallway with a small dining room. A large length of black cloth has been fixed to the wall at the back of the dining room. Since no light is falling on this background, any creases in the cloth are hidden. The narrowness of the hall means that the main light has to come from the front, with the lighting stand only just out-of-view of the lens. The illumination is quite soft because a lot of light is being reflected onto the subject from the hall walls and ceiling. Since the doorway is in the middle of the dining room wall, it is possible to use backlighting from either side without any risk of flare in the lens – the doorframe acts as a giant lens hood. Despite the limitations, the pictures show that there is plenty of scope for producing a wide range of different shots by altering backgrounds, poses and props.

One of the biggest problems facing the home photographer is the lack of studio length. Width is not so critical – even four or five feet is adequate for some pictures, providing you have the length. Being able to move the camera back from the subject means that you can use a longer lens. This generally gives a more pleasing perspective to the picture. (Strictly speaking, it's not the focal length of the lens but the distance from the subject which governs perspective, though in a home studio the two usually go together.)

But while space in front of the subject is a luxury, space behind the subject is a necessity. Although there are some occasions when the subject can be close to the background, you have much more scope for creative lighting techniques if there is an open area behind the subject.

Backlighting, for example, needs to be at least a few feet behind and to the side of the subject to be angled effectively. And if you are hoping for a totally black background, the backlights must be several feet in front of the paper or cloth to avoid any overspill of light. Even with black material, some of the light falling on the surface will be reflected and will record on the film as an unpleasant dark green tint.

With table-top subjects, three or four feet of open space in front of and behind the subject is often enough, so you can shoot successfully in a room under eight feet square. But with portraits, five or six feet in front of and behind the subject is better. Houses with a through lounge may be able to accommodate this length of studio, but you are going to be short of space in houses with smaller rooms. Unless, that is, you use two rooms. This idea will work in almost any house. You simply place your subject in the doorway between two open areas. The background is positioned in the room behind the subject. The camera is positioned in the room (or a hallway) in front of the subject. There is plenty of space in both rooms for setting up the flash units. (Avoid blocking the doorway completely with the subject unless you have alternative access to the second room, since you will need to move back and forth to arrange the lights.)

Apart from giving you more space, you will find that the doorway studio offers other advantages. First, backlighting becomes easier, since the walls on either side of the door act as baffles, shielding the direct light from the camera lens. It's actually very difficult to produce flare with this set up. Second, it is possible to position the background eight or ten feet behind the subject, so producing jet black tones on prints or slides becomes easy. Third, the narrow doorway restricts and frames the subject. This is particularly useful for portrait photography, where the doorframe can be used as part of the picture, or as a prop to aid posing.

A first sight, the doorway studio might appear to have severe limitations, but these can be used to advantage. In many cases the pictures need give no indication that they have been taken in confined conditions. And it is possible to use the doorframe to support props and accessories that would be difficult to position in the centre of a room. If you are having problems finding space to shoot, the doorway studio could be your answer.

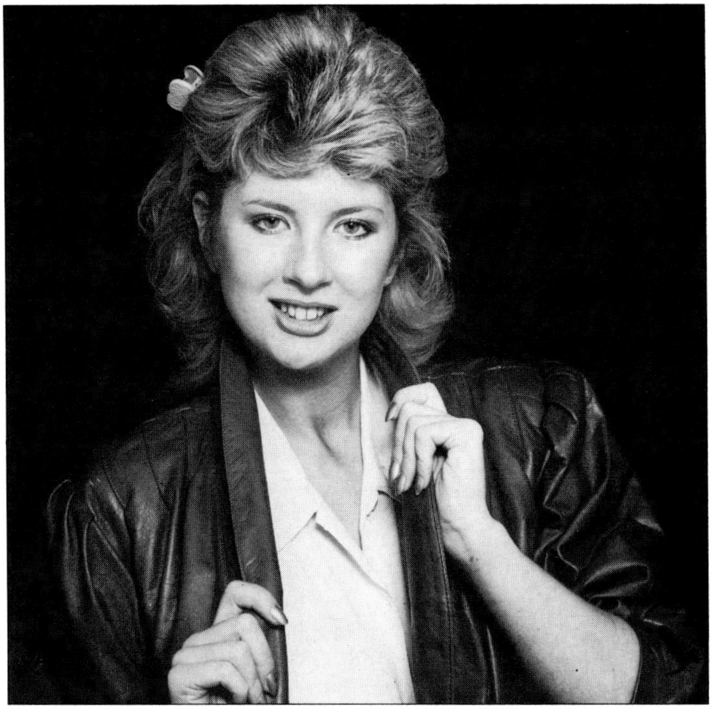

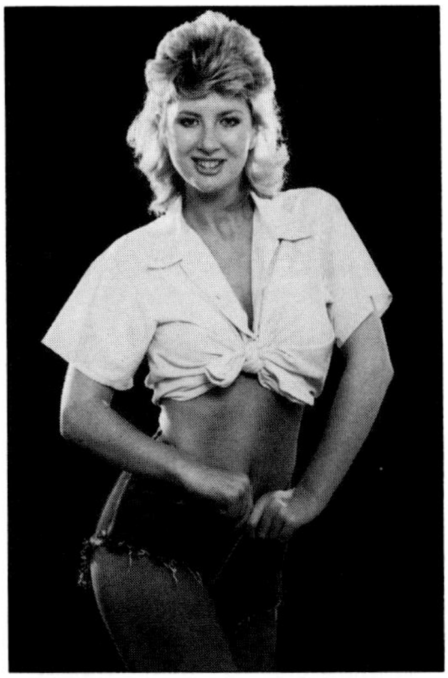

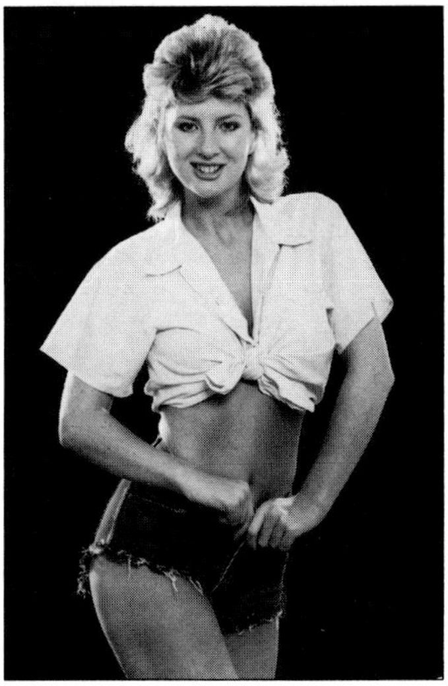

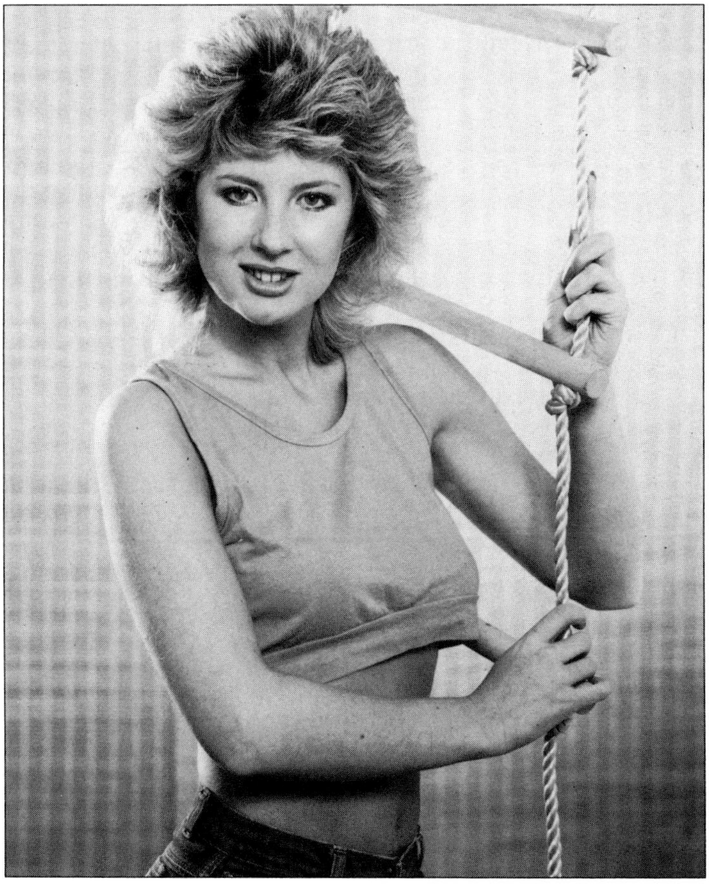

Above: One problem with lighting your subject in a doorway can be the rapid fall-off of light from head to toe. If the flash unit is used several feet above the camera *(one of the best positions)*, you may find that the lower parts of your subject take on a muddy appearance *(top)*. If you are shooting in black-and-white, and have your own darkroom, it is fairly simple to shade the image during enlarging to give a more even tone *(above)*.

Top left: The doorway studio is ideal for head-and-shoulder portraits.

Left: Use the door frame to support props – such as this rope ladder. A single nail at the top of the frame is all that's needed.

THE STUDIO EXTENSION

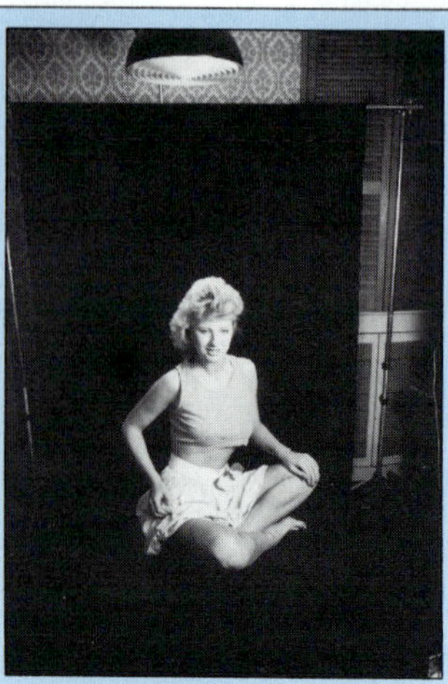

If you don't believe the photographs opposite could have been taken in a tiny studio space, take a look at the picture above. It shows a girl and background in a small dining room. A roll-film camera, fitted with a 150mm lens, is several feet down the linking hallway. If you look closely, you'll see a lampshade hanging down from the centre of the ceiling in the room. This might appear to be in the way, but it's actually being used to mask the backlight which is positioned behind and above the background cloth. This backlight is giving an attractive rim of light around the hair of the girl, but little direct light from the flash unit is reaching the lens. The picture below shows the above scene photographed by the roll-film camera.

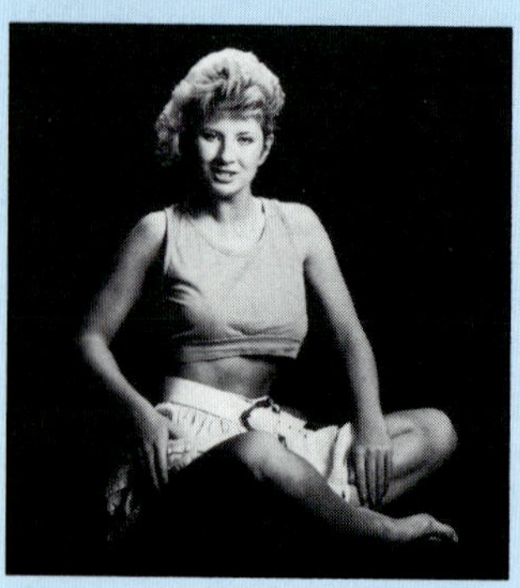

The last few pages have looked at ways of taking photographs in very small areas around the home. But while you may be content to start by shooting head-and-shoulder portraits, there will be times when you want to include all of a portrait or glamour subject in your pictures. It's not difficult, providing you are prepared to work within certain limitations.

The photographs on these two pages were taken in a small dining room with a working area of about 12 feet by 12 feet. Well, that's not strictly true. The models and all the lights were in this area, but the camera and tripod were positioned in the hall leading to the room. The set-up is really a variation of the doorway studio *(see previous page)*, but with the subject posing in the room, rather than in the doorway.

If you saw the space available, you probably wouldn't even short-list it as an area for taking full-length pictures. It appears too cramped. But what you see isn't important – it is the camera view which counts. When you are searching for studio areas in your home, always have your camera close at hand, so that you can isolate the scene from the areas which will not appear in the picture. A telephoto lens, while not essential, will certainly help, since you will need a smaller area of background than with a standard lens (that's because the angle-of-view is narrower with a telephoto lens).

A hallway running into a room is only one example of a studio extension. Two rooms linked together are just as good, with the camera in one and the studio in the other. Don't worry if the linking doorway is not central – a small studio set-up is just as good at the edge of a room as in the middle, since you will probably only have light coming from one side. If there is no space for a reflector on the opposite side, hang a white cloth from the wall. Even a room with a doorway going onto a landing can provide an extra two or three feet of shooting distance which will make all the difference to your pictures.

The main limitation of the compact studio is that it's very difficult to produce a successful full-length picture if your subject is standing. However, this is only partly because of the space needed. In many cases, it would be possible to frame all of the subject in the viewfinder, especially if a standard lens was fitted to the camera. The problem is lighting a full-length standing figure, since the flash unit will usually be positioned above head height. The fall-off of light from the head to the feet will be considerable *(see example on previous page)*. If you have several flash units, a second head can be positioned at waist height to light the lower half of the body – a low-level mounting bracket is available so that the two flash heads can be fitted to one stand. But then you have the problem of setting up large backgrounds, especially if you don't want the division between backdrop and floor to be obvious.

All these problems can be overcome by posing your subject in a compact shape to suit your compact studio. The pictures on these pages provide some ideas, but there are many variations on the same theme. And you'll find that these poses make much better use of your film formats than full-length standing shots.

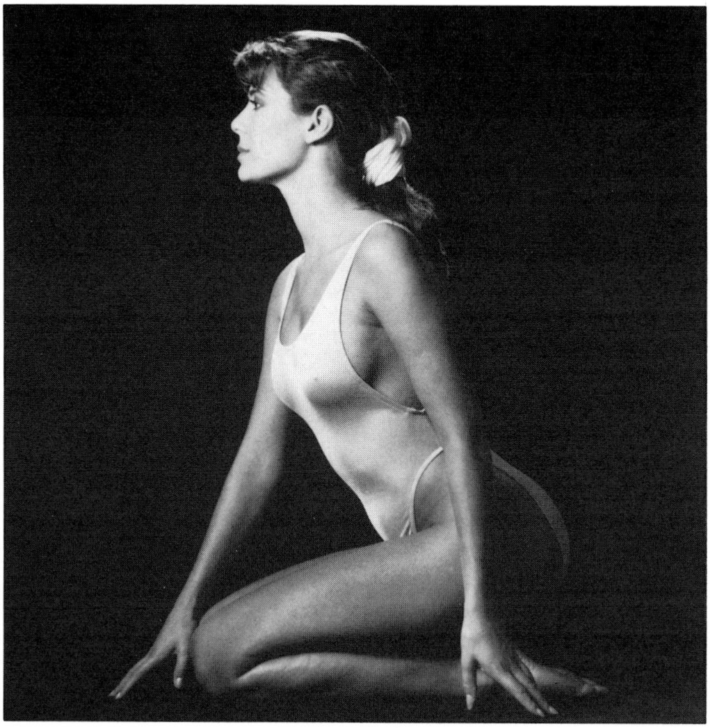

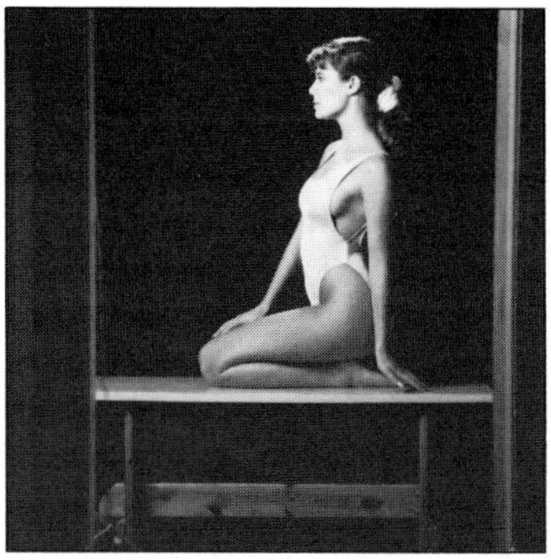

Above left: The floor is rarely a good posing surface. It creates problems with the division between foreground and background. Tables, on the other hand, are often too high for a small studio. In this picture, two benches have been pushed together and covered with a dark cloth. The small picture *(above top)* shows the set-up. A black background is not essential for compact studio shots, but it helps to avoid problems with background shadows.

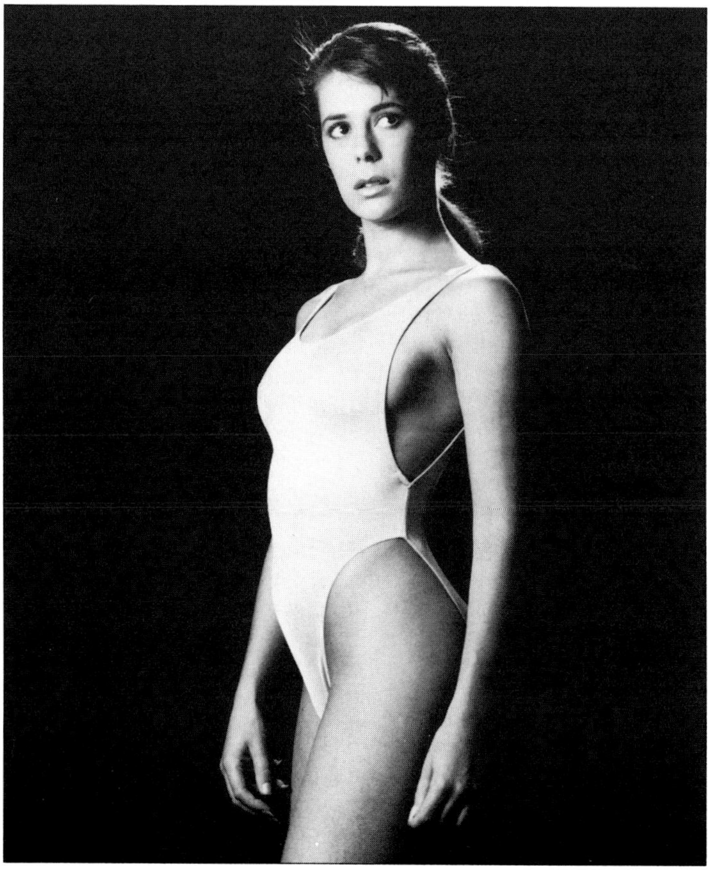

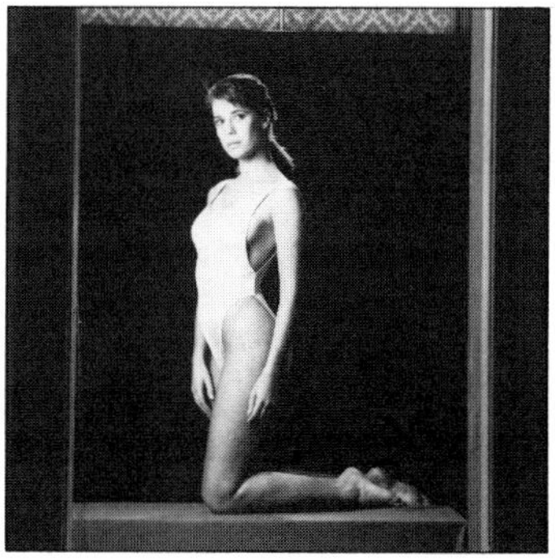

Left: You might think that the girl was standing for this pose. In fact, the studio space was not big enough – the top of the background showed in standing shots. So the girl was positioned on a low platform *(see small picture above)*. If you keep in mind that only the view seen by the camera is important, you'll be able to produce a wide range of pictures which look as if they have been taken in professional studios.

THE STAIRCASE STUDIO

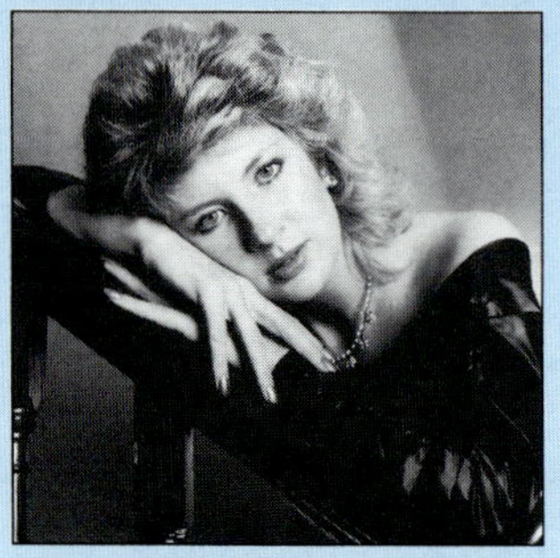

Every area on and around the staircase can be used for your pictures. Here, the banister provides an angled support for a head-and-shoulders portrait.

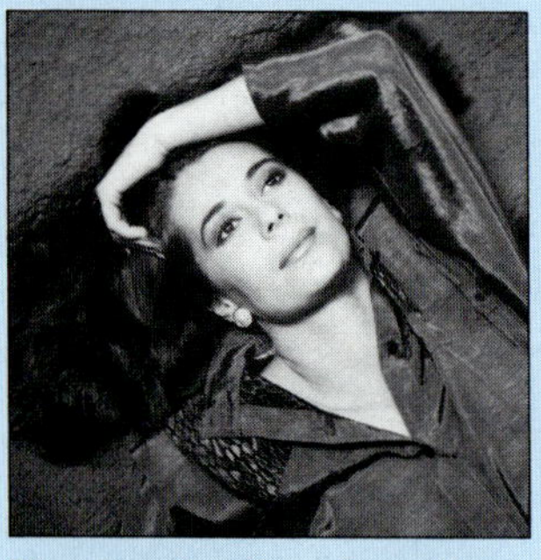

Try shooting down from the landing onto the stairs. A length of background cloth can be spread over the stairs if you want to hide the carpet or paintwork.

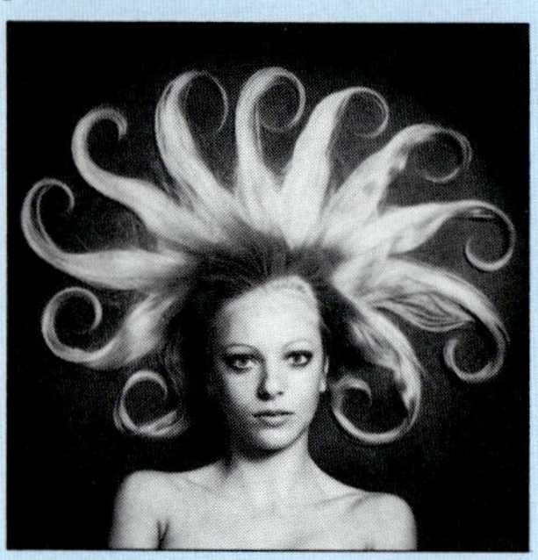

The high viewpoint offered by a staircase is ideal for a shot like this. The girl had to lay motionless for about 20 minutes while her hair was arranged and photographed.

Visit a good professional studio and one of the main features you will notice is the height of the shooting area. Vertical space can be just as important as horizontal space when it comes to taking studio shots. A high ceiling means that lights can be positioned to shine over tall backgrounds, or can be arranged directly above the subject. Alternatively, you can place your subject on a platform for a low-angle shot, or support the camera 15 or 20 feet from the ground for a high viewpoint.

The average home has a ceiling height of around 8 to 10 feet, so many of these techniques might appear impossible. But there is one area of most houses which offers increased height – the staircase. You might think that the hall, stairs and any landing area are too narrow or cramped for photography. However, if you take a look through your camera viewfinder, you may change your mind – particularly if your main interest is portrait or glamour photography.

First, the staircase offers an excellent posing platform. The steps offer a seat, plus rests for arms and legs, all at different levels. Your subject can be placed in the centre of the treads, leaning forwards, or can be at the side, leaning against the wall. (Avoid shots with people leaning back — they lack any impact.) And you can vary the shots by positioning your subject so that they are near the bottom of the stairs, on a level with the camera, or further up the stairs, looking down on the camera. Of course, you won't usually want the stair carpet and wallpaper competing for attention in the pictures, but a large length of plain cloth draped around the area will give a pleasant neutral background.

With a wall on one side and a stair rail on the other, there is not a lot of room to position the flash units. However, one unit behind and above the camera will give a good main light, while a backlight can be placed at the top of the stairs, shining down. In many cases, the bottom of the lighting stand will be higher than the top of the subject, so you will not have to worry about the stand appearing in any of your photographs.

Your staircase studio can also be used for high angle shots. Here, the subject is in the hall (or on the first landing if there are two flights of stairs). You stand on the stairs, holding the camera over the rail, to look down on the scene. If you are only taking a few shots, and do not need a viewpoint immediately above the subject, a handheld camera is adequate. However, if you are taking a sequence of pictures, or want to keep the camera central and square to the subject, some type of support is almost essential. If you intend to use the staircase area frequently for photography, you might be able to screw a discreet panel to the ceiling and fix an upside-down ball-and-socket head when needed. But check that this is very secure. And if you are photographing people, make sure that you have adequate third party liability insurance, just in case there are any accidents. Public liability insurance is cheap, and is often included in general household policies. However, check the small print to make sure it covers hobbies. And if you are taking pictures with the intention of selling them, you'll need professional cover. Ask your insurance broker for details.

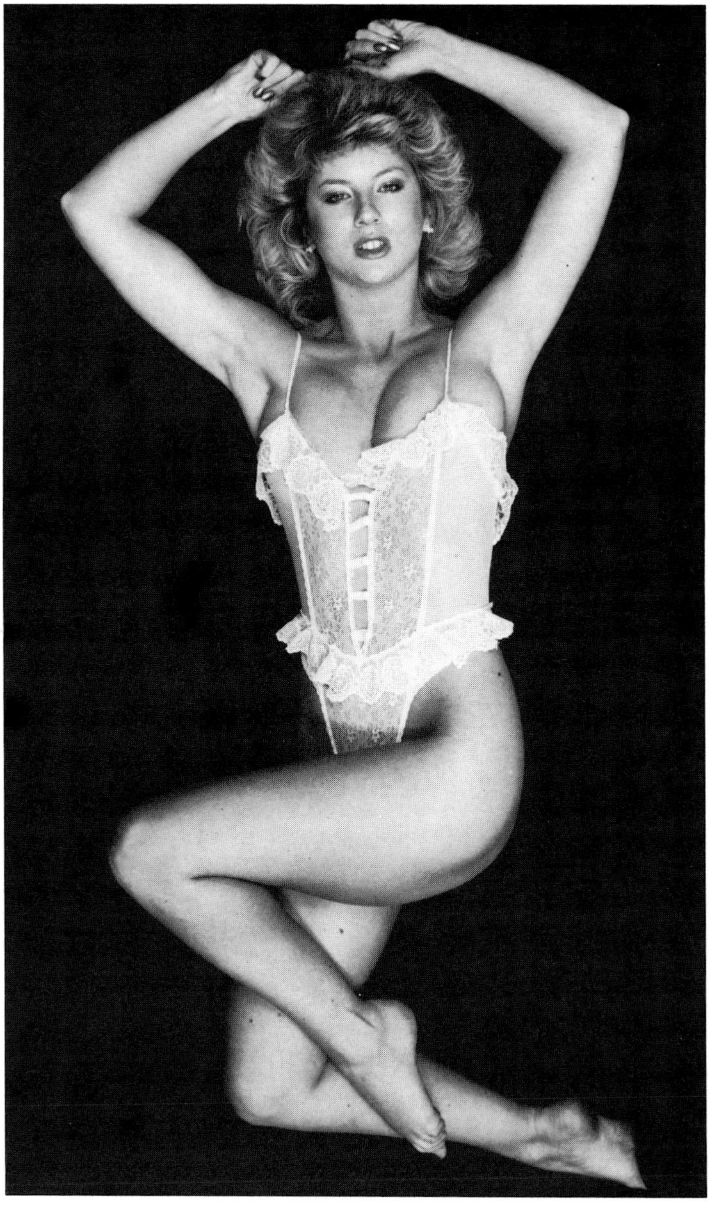

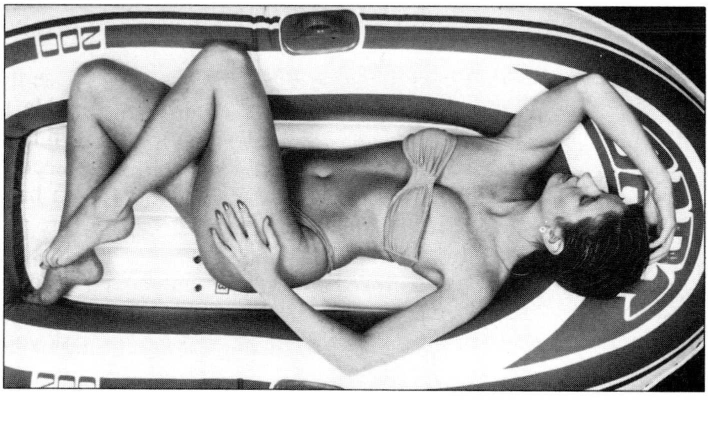

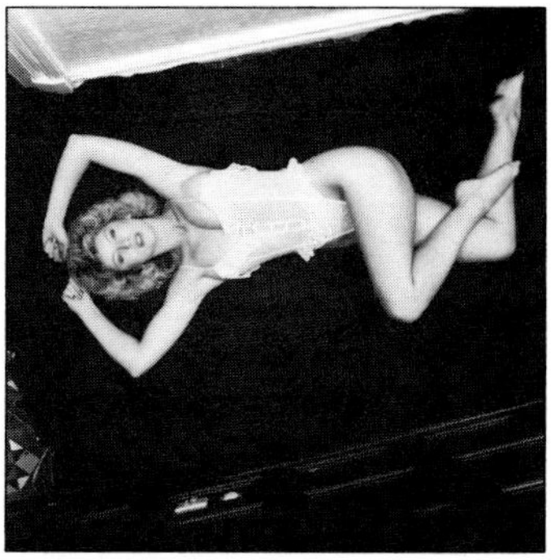

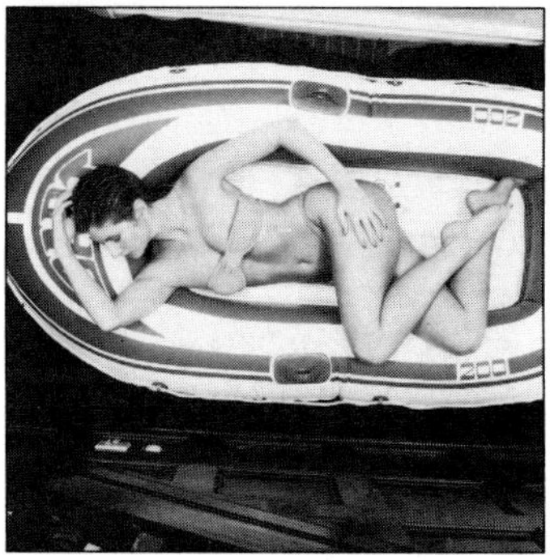

Above and left: It is surprising how little space is needed to take glamour pictures. The floor area for the pictures on the left is in a hall just 45 inches wide. The pictures above show the full area seen by the camera – including the wall and the side of the staircase. In both cases, a roll-film camera has been used, with a standard 80mm lens. By standing halfway up the stairs, it was possible to hold the camera against the ceiling of the hall. A waist-level finder helped with the focusing. The lighting was very simple – just two flash units, one at either end of the model, but aimed at the white ceiling so that only reflected light is reaching the subject. The flash heads were angled carefully so that no direct light from the flash tubes reached the camera lens. Both pictures show the same girl, first with her normal hairstyle, and then after she has combed setting gel through it. Since the camera is immediately overhead, there is no right or wrong way up for the pictures – they can be displayed as you wish.

THE GARAGE STUDIO

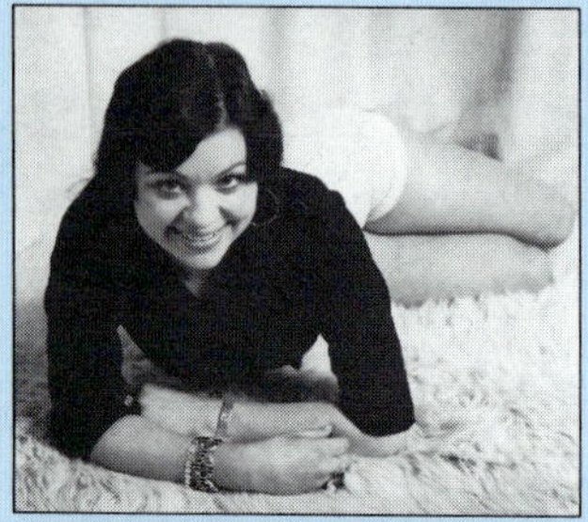

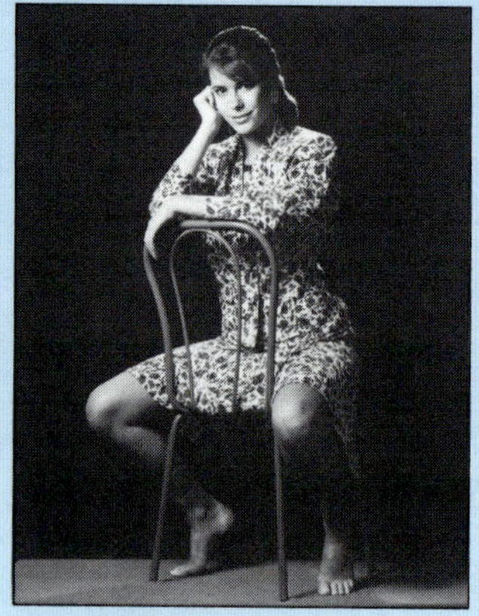

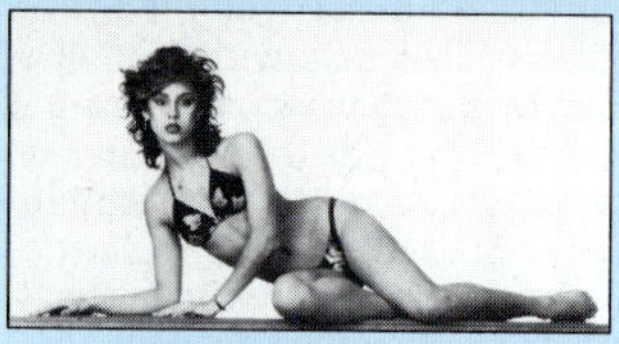

Your garage pictures do not need to look as if they have been taken in a garage. It's easy to set up some curtains and a rug (top), a black background and a chair (centre), or a well-lit white background (bottom). All of these shots were taken with the camera four feet from the ground, or less, overcoming any problem of a low roof height. And by posing the model on or close to the ground, the backlight used for the centre shot could still be about five feet above the head.

Which is the largest clear area inside your home? The chances are that it is the garage — providing you have left the car outside, of course. This space is easy to turn into a temporary studio, and it is one of the areas least likely to disturb other members of the household. If may also be one of the few areas you can leave set up overnight, as long as the car does not object to a night in the open.

The most obvious disadvantage of many modern garages is the low roof. However, as with all home studio problems, this is simply a challenge to be overcome. For table-top photography, the lack of height is not a major problem. For portraits, the answer is to work closer to the ground. Don't take head-and-shoulder pictures with the subject standing. Sit them on a chair, or even on the floor. And then lower your camera position so that the lens is still about level with the face. This will let you position a flash unit several feet above head height, so that it is a perfect backlight.

It's still possible to include all of your subject in a portrait or glamour shot, even if the ceiling is only seven feet high. Although full-length standing shots are almost impossible, there are plenty of attractive sitting, kneeling and crouching poses which reduce the effective height of the person, and which will give an image more suited to the shape of your camera format.

Although you can bring tables and chairs from the house to your garage studio, this may not be very convenient. Instead, buy one or two foldaway chairs and stools from your local furniture store. An inexpensive trestle table is also very useful. More expensive, but a good investment, is a tubular construction kit. There is at least one version available, designed for children, which uses red plastic tubes of various lengths, with black plastic corner pieces and black square inserts. This can be used to build small table tops, rigid posing platforms, simple steps, and many other useful props.

The main advantage of a garage studio is that you probably don't have to leave it in the condition you found it! If you want a red background for a table-top shot, it's probably just as easy to paint an area of one of the walls as it is to find and support a suitable backdrop. Cans of aerosol paint make a colour change quick and easy. If you don't want to apply paint direct to a wall, buy a large sheet of hardboard and colour this instead.

No one is likely to complain about hooks and clamps, either. Rather than use all your flash units on lighting stands, you may be able to fasten suitable supports to side walls, giving a less cluttered floor space. Overhead beams can be used for backlights. A wall-mounted background paper support can be a permanent fixture at one end of the garage. A row of large nails along one of the walls can be used to hold some of the lighting accessories, such as barndoors, honeycombs and synchronization cables. All these features will help you to make the most of the available space, and also mean that the area can be converted from garage to studio in a matter of minutes.

Don't leave your flash units or camera equipment in the garage unless you are sure it is really secure. If the garage is separate from the house, it is worth fitting a loud burglar alarm even if equipment is only left there during the day.

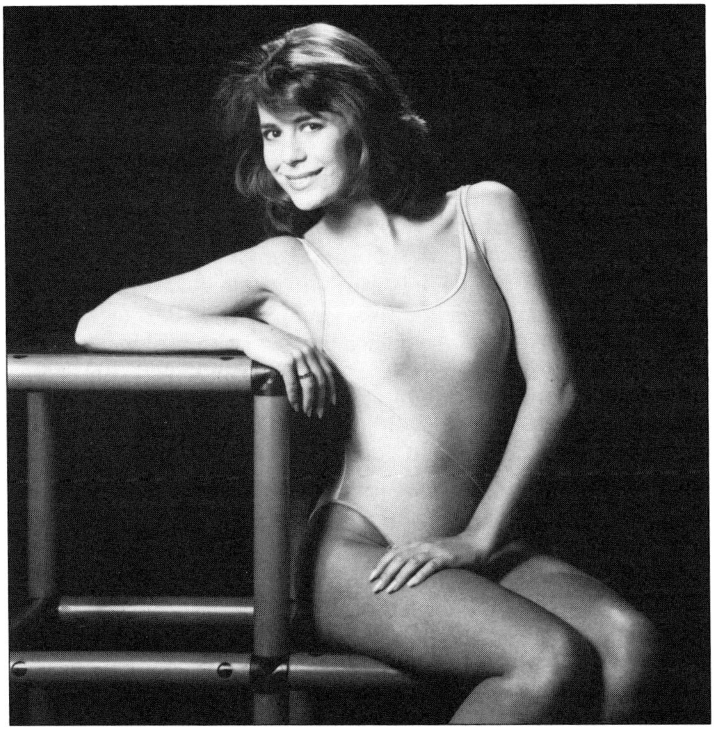

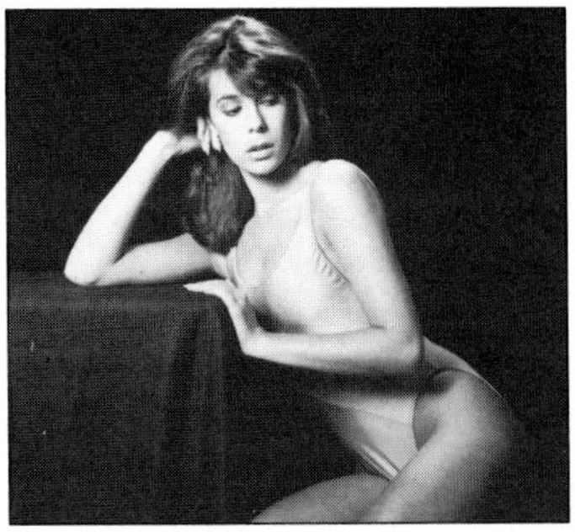

Above and left: An extremely useful accessory for the garage studio (or any other studio area with enough space) is a strong children's climbing frame. It can be assembled into a variety of posing platforms and used with or without a cloth drape.

Below: A low roof in a garage should be a challenge, rather than a problem. It will encourage you to find poses which can be taken at or near floor level. Here, the model is posing on a length of white paper which has been laid on the floor.

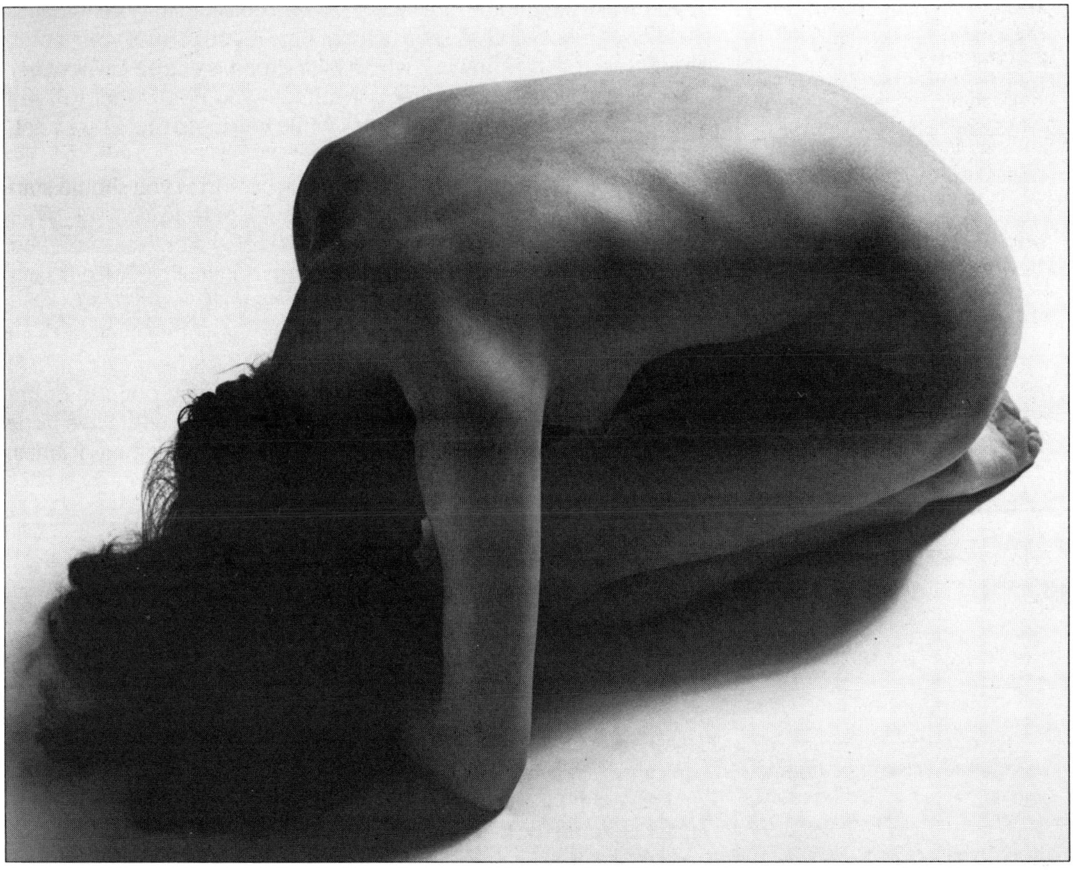

STUDIO WORKBOX

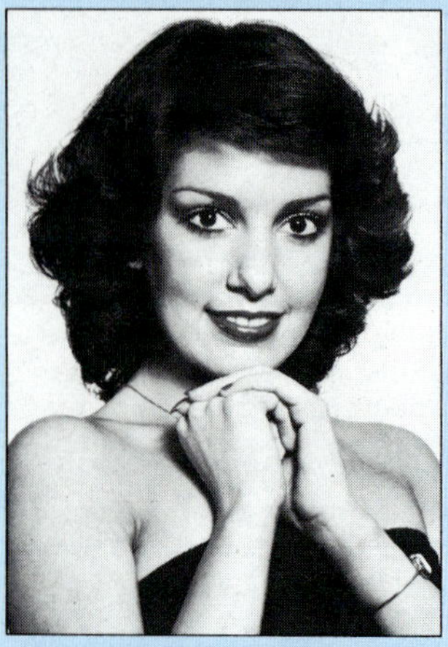

Make-up does not normally concern most amateur photographers. When shooting female portraits or glamour pictures, they tend to assume that the subject will know what to do. To some extent, this is probably correct, and few photographers will know enough about make-up to offer any advice. But it is worth reading a couple of books on the subject, so that you can use the right words if you want the make-up altered. It is also worth collecting a variety of useful make-up items, since few models will carry everything in their own kit. Lip gloss is particularly useful – it gives an attractive wet-look to the lips. Also recommended is a theatrical blending powder (in case the subject begins to perspire under the lamps). And most glamour photographers keep a bottle of baby oil to make the model's skin glisten in bikini, topless and nude shots.

Opposite: A selection of props and accessories from a photographer's workbox and store cupboard.

You will soon discover that a great many everyday household items are invaluable for home studio photography. Even a simple table-top arrangement can make use of lengths of string, Blu-tack, drawing pins, clothes pegs, rubber bands and fuse wire. After a couple of studio sessions spent hunting down these items, you will realise that what you need is a studio workbox. Although a shoe box might be adequate for a short while, it is worth investing in an attractive box with plenty of compartments. Take your pick from the range of tool boxes on display in do-it-yourself stores, or the foldout sewing boxes found in the haberdashery section of a department store. Always buy a box which looks twice as big as the one you think you'll need.

Start your workbox off by raiding drawers and cupboards for a selection of anything that looks of practical use. And when you go in search of special items for a particular session, put them in the workbox after use, rather than returning them to their original location. You will know that your workbox is well-stocked when you start going to it for household items.

In addition to the workbox, you will need space for all the lengths of cloth, sheets of card, and other studio accessories you start to acquire. You will probably have to spread these around the house and in the garage, but try to keep them in as few places as possible. If you are in the middle of a studio session and suddenly decide that you need a black cloth, it saves a lot of time if you can put your hands straight on it. And knowing where everything is can be particularly important if you are shooting portraits — you don't want to keep your subject waiting for 15 minutes while you try to find a straw hat, or pair of lace gloves.

Hats and gloves are just some of the accessories you should start to buy if you are going to specialise in portrait and glamour photography. Although your subjects will bring along some of their own clothes, there will be many occasions when an item from your own store adds just the splash of colour needed.

You should also have a range of simple 'props' that can be used to add interest and help with different poses. Furniture stores will provide a range of cheap folding stools and chairs, often in bright colours. Children's departments in large stores will have rope ladders, paddling pools, inflatable boats and climbing frames. Games departments will offer colourful weight training accessories. Clothing stores will sell you shorts and t-shirts.

Table-top photography is also easier if you have a large range of miscellaneous oddments stored in boxes. Whenever you are out shopping, look for interesting items that might form part of a photograph, or which can be used in constructing sets. Bring back jars of sand, pebbles and shells from a visit to the seaside. Collect dry leaves, grasses and twigs during an afternoon walk in the country. Keep the polystyrene pieces that are using for packing. Buy cans of spray snow and lengths of gold and silver tinsel at Christmas. It is also worth getting to know the shops in your area that sell antiques and secondhand goods. It is often possible to hire interesting and unusual items for two or three days to use in your studio pictures.

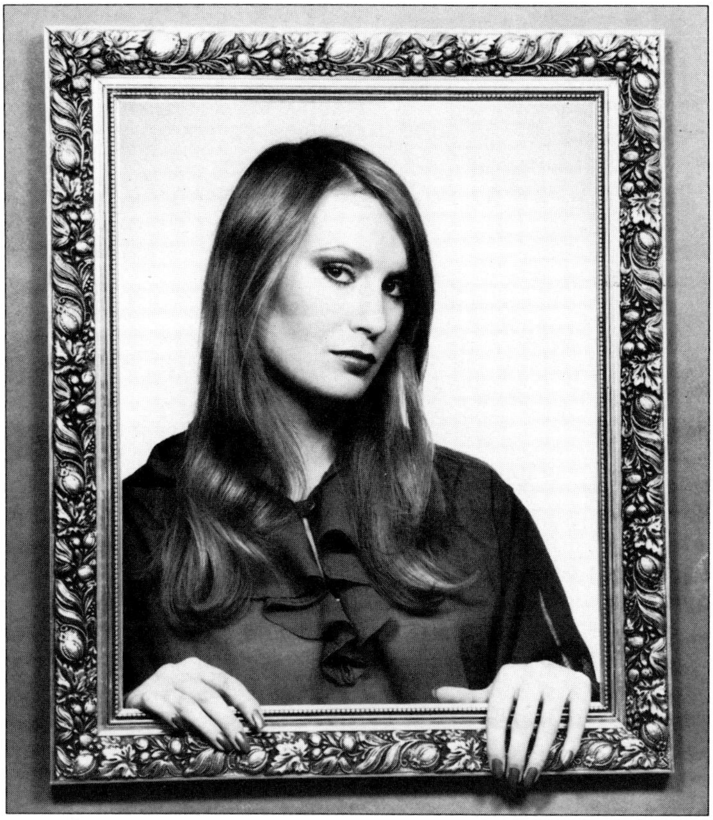
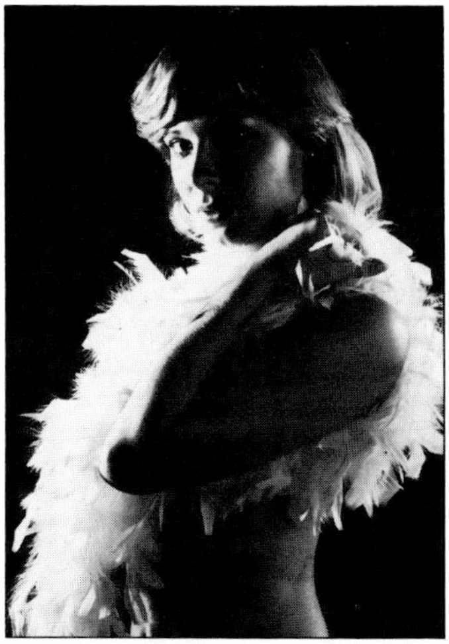
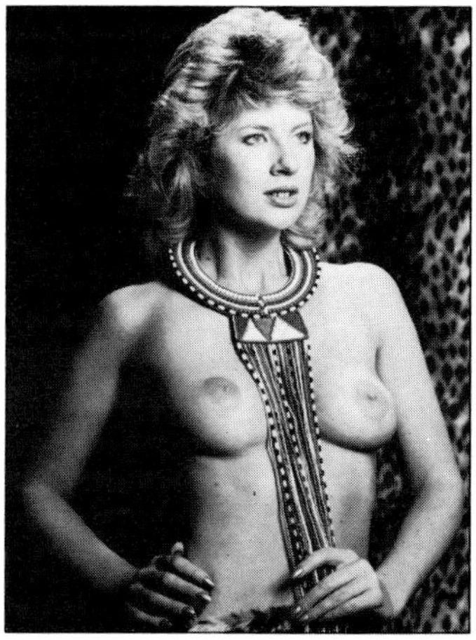
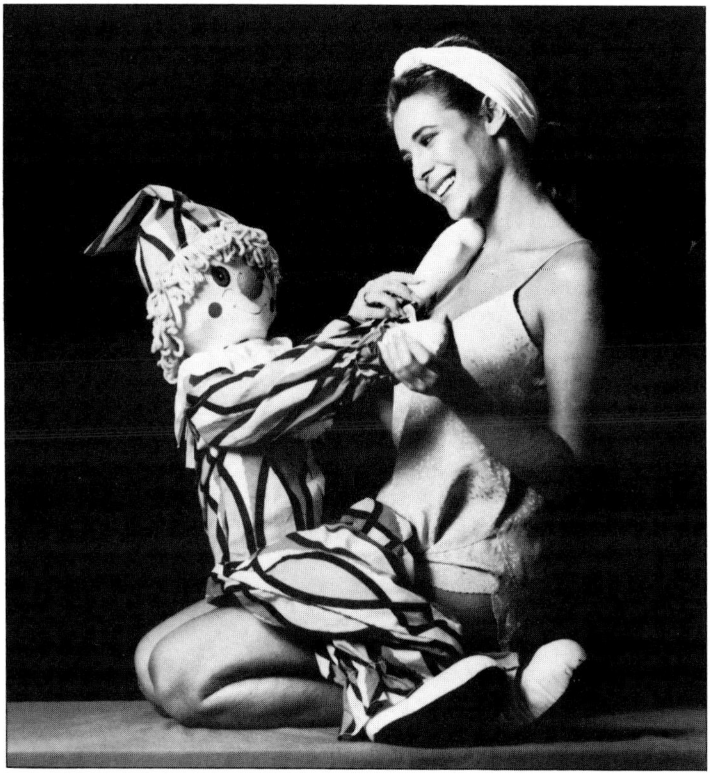
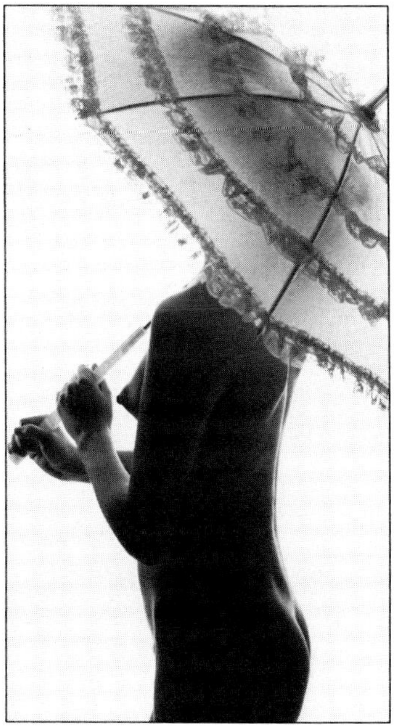

INDEX